Stan Jackson BSc Hons

Congratulations

on your

degree

With love from

Debs & Kevin

xx

5th June 2004

Shark

BBC
BOOKS

Shark

Mark Carwardine

For Miranda and Jemma, with love

Published by BBC Books, BBC Worldwide Ltd,
Woodlands, 80 Wood Lane, London W12 0TT

First published 2004 © BBC Worldwide Ltd
Copyright © Mark Carwardine 2004
The moral right of the author has been asserted.

ISBN 0 563 48723 2

Editorial director: Shirley Patton
Project editor: Patricia Burgess
Art director: Linda Blakemore
Designer: Annette Peppis

Picture researcher: Frances Abraham
Illustrator: Ian Coleman
Indexer: Helen Snaith
Production controller: Arlene Alexander

Set in Officina by BBC Worldwide Limited
Printed and bound in Singapore by Tien Wah Press
Colour separations by Radstock Reproductions, Midsomer Norton

ILLUSTRATIONS, PAGES 1–6
Pages 1 and 2: Giant whale shark.
Page 3: Scalloped hammerheads.
Page 5: Blacktip shark.
Page 6: Great white shark.

If you require further information about any BBC Worldwide
product call 08700 777 001 or visit our website on
www.bbcshop.com

Contents

Introduction

I'll never forget my first close encounter with a wild shark. It was May 1990 and I was diving on the Great Barrier Reef in Australia, when a whitetip reef shark swam past. It was considerably smaller than me and quite clearly minding its own business. Far from coming to investigate, let alone taking an exploratory bite, it disappeared into the murk as soon as I turned and swam towards it.

You could hardly describe those few seconds with one of the world's more unassuming sharks as a face-to-face encounter with a deadly super-predator, but it was a moment I will always remember. In the years since then I have been fortunate enough to dive with a huge number of sharks of many different species, and watching them has become a lifelong passion.

Only a generation ago, anyone diving with sharks was considered mad, reckless or outrageously adventurous. But now we know better. We know that sharks are by no means the empty-headed monsters portrayed by Hollywood, and aren't anywhere near as dangerous as decades of media hype would have us believe. We can swim with them after all – and live to tell the tale. Good sense is at last beginning to prevail.

As we open our eyes to real sharks instead of the fictional ones in our imagination, it's hard not to be impressed. In one form or another, they have inhabited our seas and oceans for more than 400 million years. They witnessed the rise of our own species – and may be around for long enough to witness our downfall, too. Their long swim up the evolutionary ladder has turned them into highly efficient predators armed with formidable weaponry. And they are equipped with such a sophisticated and awe-inspiring array of sensory mechanisms that we can barely imagine the world as they experience it. Some might even argue that sharks are better adapted to living in their world than we are in ours.

Talking about 'sharks' is rather like talking about 'mammals': it implies that they are all the same. But they are not. Hammerheads and cookie-cutter sharks, for instance, are as different as whales and rabbits. They come in a mind-boggling variety of shapes, sizes and colours, ranging from tiny lantern and pygmy sharks, small enough to fit in a human hand, to gargantuan whale sharks, which are larger than many of their namesakes in the mammalian world. Also, they include some of the most remarkable creatures on the planet. Who could fail to be impressed by the basking shark – essentially an industrial-sized mouth with fins? Or the formidable great white, with its powerful jaws, large, triangular teeth and jet-black eyes? Or the tasselled wobbegong that spends much of its life pretending to be a seaweed-encrusted rock?

The aim of this book is to introduce these and many other weird and wonderful sharks. It describes their origins and ancestors, introduces the diversity of sharks and the way they are classified, analyses their perfectly designed bodies, explains how they reproduce, investigates sharks as the ultimate killing machines, and puts our irrational fear of them into perspective. There is a chapter on where and how sharks are being studied, together with some of the latest scientific findings. Perhaps most important of all, there is a plea for the sharks themselves, as more than 100 million of them are killed by people every year. They are in serious trouble and need all the help they can get. For us to wipe them out – through greed, need, sheer recklessness or simple ignorance – would be a tragedy.

The final chapter is an introduction to shark watching. This is included in the hope that, after reading the book, you will feel encouraged to jump into the sea for a real-life close encounter with one of the most beautiful, awe-inspiring and mysterious creatures on Earth. If you do, you won't be disappointed.

Mark Carwardine

August 2003

How long have sharks been around?

When did people first study sharks?

Why are sharks so feared?

Are all sharks equally dangerous?

How are sharks classified?

Do all sharks live in the same habitat?

How many species of shark are there?

What characteristics do sharks have in common?

Which is the most ancient order of sharks?

How many orders are there?

The World of Sharks

Awe-inspiring Animals

Sharks are probably the most maligned, misunderstood and feared creatures on the planet. Synonymous with danger, they seem to provoke an irrational fear in us that is based on an entirely distorted view of their lives and habits. However, they are not the sinister, mindless killing machines the film industry and popular press would have us believe. They may be impressive and sophisticated predators at the top of the marine food chain, but the vast majority of them are not intent on hurting people. Statistically, even if you spend a great deal of time in the sea, the likelihood of being attacked by a shark is very small indeed.

The bottom line is this: sharks possess such acute senses, they are such powerful hunters and they have such a wide distribution that few people would emerge from the sea unharmed if they really were out to get us. The truth is that they are not out to get us at all.

Admittedly, it is hard to describe sharks as lovable. And in human terms they do have some undeniably nasty habits. They can regurgitate their food by turning their stomachs inside out, for example, and if unborn pups are not eaten by their brothers and sisters inside the womb, there is every chance that their mother will eat them as soon as they are born. But scientific studies of sharks reveal them to be awe-inspiring animals more worthy of respect than fear or horror. Marvels of evolutionary engineering, they have bodies that boat-builders can only envy, and wide-ranging sensory systems that are so 'technologically advanced' they leave human experts gasping.

In one form or another, sharks have inhabited the Earth's oceans for about 400 million years. Their ancestors survived no fewer than five mass extinctions – including one 245 million years ago, when 96 per cent of all marine life was wiped out. They witnessed the rise and fall of the dinosaurs, and had evolved into near-perfect predators by the time mammals returned to the sea.

It is not surprising that they have been an endless source of fascination since time immemorial. Shark teeth and skins have been found in Maltese ruins that were occupied more than 4000 years ago, and sharks appear prominently in myths and legends dating back centuries. Around the world they have, on the one hand, been worshipped as gods bringing good fortune to seafarers, and on the other hand, believed to be spirits sent by sorcerers to bring death and ill fortune. Nowadays, they are an endless source of fascination and wonder for scientists trying to understand how sharks live in their underwater world.

Studying sharks

The first scientific study of sharks was probably made by the Greek naturalist Aristotle (384–322 BC). He travelled around the Mediterranean, researching the local wildlife, and produced a ground-breaking work called *Historia Animalium*. Many of his observations on sharks were surprisingly accurate and perceptive. He recognized that they differed from other fishes by having rough skin instead of relatively smooth skin, and by having skeletons made of cartilage instead of bone.

Our knowledge of sharks since Aristotle's time has increased less than might be imagined. From a human perspective, they live in a relatively hostile, inaccessible environment, so they are difficult animals to study. For centuries their lives were shrouded in mystery, and even today, we are not entirely sure how many species there are, let alone how most of them live. Captive sharks and dead ones caught by fishermen have helped us to gain a significant amount of basic knowledge, but the real challenge now is to understand the habits and behaviour of sharks living wild and free.

Observing sharks in their own underwater world was not really possible until the 1940s, when Jacques-Yves Cousteau (in collaboration with engineer Emile Gagnon) designed and tested the aqualung. This was a predecessor to the scuba system now used by divers across the globe, and it opened up a whole new underwater world to shark researchers, enabling them to study their subjects face to face. In recent years, researchers have also benefited from sophisticated high-tech equipment, such as radio and satellite tags, which are extending the boundaries of shark research still further.

Page 8: Blue sharks are among the most attractive and graceful of the world's sharks.
Opposite: The great white shark is the ultimate super-predator.
Right: Shark attacks have fascinated for generations, as in *Watson and the Shark* by John Singleton Copley.

Sharks and people

Modern scientific studies are revealing an entirely different side to sharks – one that is more intriguing than intimidating. But the worldwide hatred and fear of them is so deeply entrenched that it is likely to be many years before most of us become more rational in our attitude towards them.

The trend for reporting gory and sensational shark attacks was probably set as long as 2500 years ago by the Greek historian Herodotus (485–425 BC). He described a dreadful sea battle off Athos, in northeastern Greece, during which many boats sank and lots of sailors were eaten by sharks. Several centuries later, in AD 77, the Roman naturalist Pliny the Elder reported attacks on sponge fishermen. The sharks' bad reputation continued to gather momentum and, by the sixteenth century, the French naturalist Guillaume Rondelet was describing complete human bodies being removed from the stomachs of sharks, including,

on one (perhaps apocryphal) occasion, a knight in a full suit of armour.

Then, in the summer of 1916, a rogue shark struck the New Jersey shoreline in the eastern USA, killing several swimmers. Popular opinion at the time suggested that it was a great white, but the species was never properly identified, and experts today believe it was more likely to have been a bull shark. Whatever it was, it caused a sensation. President Woodrow Wilson even called a cabinet meeting to discuss ways of dealing with the 'crisis'.

Those attacks may have been a turning point in our paranoia about sharks. Reputedly, they provided the inspiration for Peter Benchley's book *Jaws* (1974), which Steven Spielberg later made into one of the most successful movies of all time. Many shark conservationists believe that *Jaws* is largely responsible for the anti-shark hysteria that has gripped the Western world ever since. Our distorted view of sharks is such that they do not 'inhabit' the world's oceans, they 'infest' them, and many people regard the only good shark as a dead one.

But public opinion is changing, albeit slowly. Even Peter Benchley himself publicly laments the impact of *Jaws* on our attitude towards sharks. In *Shark Trouble* (2002) he wrote: 'We knew so little back then, and have learned so much since, that I couldn't possibly write the same story today.' As we learn more about sharks, we are gradually seeing them for what they really are rather than what we used to think them to be – stunning rather than sinister creatures. The public image of sharks is undergoing a revolution of sorts and good sense is at last beginning to prevail. They now have some friends.

The sad fact is that they need all the friends they can get. According to the most widely accepted scientific estimate, more than 100 million sharks are killed by people every year. Many experts believe that even this figure may be an underestimate. No shark species has yet been declared extinct, although it is very likely that some have disappeared without our knowledge; several species are critically endangered and a number of regional stocks have already been wiped out.

The diversity of sharks

Talking about 'sharks' is rather like talking about 'mammals': it implies that they are all the same. But they are not. Hammerheads and cookie-cutter sharks, for instance, are as different as whales and rabbits.

Sharks come in all shapes, sizes and colours, each adapted to its own particular niche in the sea. They range from tiny dwarf dogsharks and spined pygmy sharks, which are small enough to fit in a human hand, to gargantuan whale sharks, which are larger than many of their namesakes in the mammalian world. There are typical 'movie' sharks, with sleek, torpedo-shaped bodies, tall, triangular dorsal fins and powerful scythe-shaped tails, and parasitic sharks with sucker-like mouths and enormous teeth. There are ray-like and eel-like sharks, and sharks with elongated,

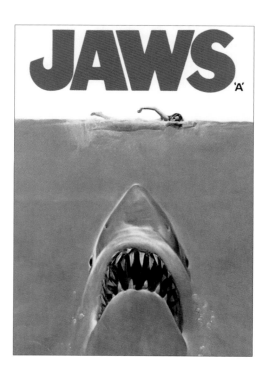

Left: Anti-shark hysteria has gripped the Western world for many years.
Opposite: Two extremes: a scalloped hammerhead (main picture) and a cookie-cutter shark (inset) demonstrate the huge variety of sharks.

flattened snouts in the shape of a paddle. There are sharks that resemble seaweed-encrusted rocks, huge sharks with cavernous mouths and thick lips, and even deep-sea sharks that glow in the dark. Some are brightly coloured, others perfectly camouflaged or rather drab, and they can be blue, white, grey, tan, brown, black, green, orange or purple, and spotted or striped.

Found in all the seas and oceans of the world, and even thousands of kilometres up some rivers, sharks live everywhere from the freezing cold waters of the poles to the warm waters of the tropics. There are sharks inhabiting coral reefs, mangrove forests, rocky shores, muddy estuaries and even the weird and wonderful world underneath the Arctic ice. They can be found swimming at the ocean surface or down in the coldest, darkest depths several kilometres below. Some live in the pounding surf close to shore, while many prefer the open ocean and swim

perpetually in mid-water, and others choose to skulk around in the ocean depths, or even lie on the seabed.

Their lifestyles are just as varied. Some sharks swim constantly and actively pursue swift and agile prey; others lie in wait ready to ambush much slower-moving prey. A few of the larger species survive by straining microscopic plankton from the sea water, while some of their close relatives bite off enormous chunks of flesh from large fish and dead whales.

Classification of sharks

Scientists classify fishes (and all other animals) into groups that share similar characteristics: the ones with more common characteristics are thought to be more closely related. The classification of fishes in general, and sharks in particular, is a

highly debated and evolving subject, and no single version is universally accepted. But the basics are fairly straightforward.

The vast majority of fishes belong to an enormous group known as the bony fishes. As their name suggests, they have bony skeletons; they also have smooth scales on their skin, a protective covering over their gills, and a swim bladder to help them maintain neutral buoyancy in the water. (Neutral buoyancy is the ability to 'hover' in the water without sinking or floating to the surface.) They range in size from huge ocean sunfish, which can weigh up to 2 tonnes (2 tons), to tiny dwarf gobies, which have average lengths of 8.6 mm (0.34 inches) for males and 8.9 mm (0.35 inches) for females. There are more than 25,000 species of bony fishes, and they make up the class Osteichthyes.

Sharks are classified in a different group of fishes, together with the rays and chimaeras, which are quite different from bony fishes in their structure, physiology and biology. They form the class Chondrichthyes, and together account for less than 5 per cent of all the world's fishes. The Chondrichthyes are known as the cartilaginous fishes, since their skeletons are made of cartilage (a tough, flexible material that is also found in human joints, such as knees and elbows). The precise number of species in this group is a matter of considerable controversy but, including some that have yet to be named, more than 1100 have been identified so far. Fewer than half of these are sharks:

Above: Rays, such as these mantas, are basically flat-bodied sharks, and the two groups share many characteristics.

Opposite: The strange-looking chimaeras, or elephantfish, are also closely related to sharks.

approximately 410 species are currently known to science. This figure is continually increasing because, on average, several new species are identified and added to the list every year. Taking into account all the sharks that have been photographed or collected, but not yet scientifically described or named, there could be as many as 450–500 species altogether.

Chimaeras are primitive, deep-water fishes now confined to sub-Arctic and Antarctic waters. Also known as ratfish, elephantfish or ghost sharks, their mouths are equipped with 'tooth plates' for crushing hard food, and they have a dorsal spine with a venom sac at the base. Some have strange, rabbit-like heads and long, whip-like tails. There are approximately 30 living species, and they form a separate sub-class known as the Holocephali.

It is hard to believe that the predominantly flat, slow-moving rays are related to the generally faster, streamlined sharks. But they share many characteristics, and sharks and rays are grouped together in the sub-class Elasmobranchii (they are often referred to as elasmobranchs). Rays are basically flat-bodied sharks, with their gill slits on the underside, and have two relatively large pectoral fins; most swim by flapping or undulating these great pectorals. There are nearly 500 species of rays and their relatives (skates, sawfish and torpedos), and together they

form the order Rajiformes. Sharks tend to be cylinder-shaped, with their gill slits on the sides, and have two relatively small pectoral fins; they swim by moving their heads from side to side, sending 'waves' down to their tails to make it swing from side to side too (they also swing the tail itself). But there are exceptions, and some members of the two groups can easily be confused. Pacific angel sharks have flattened, ray-like bodies, for example, while certain rays, such as guitarfishes and sawfishes, swim with the help of lateral movements of their tails like sharks.

There are eight main groups, or orders, of sharks.

Order Hexanchiformes

Two families: Chlamydoselachidae and Hexanchidae
Species: Sixgill, sevengill, frilled and cow sharks
This is believed to be the most primitive, or ancient, group of sharks. The family Chlamydoselachidae contains just one living species, known as the frilled (or frill) shark, so named because of the frill-like covers to its gill slits. It lives in deep water near the seabed. There are six gill slits on each side (most other sharks have only five), and only one dorsal fin. Its jaws and teeth resemble fossil species from 350 million years ago. In the family Hexanchidae there are five species, which include the sixgill, sevengill and cow (or comb-toothed) sharks. They also live in

deep water and have six or seven gill slits on each side and one dorsal fin. Their jaws and vertebrae resemble their fossil counterparts from 190 million years ago.

Order Heterodontiformes

One family: Heterodontidae

Species: Port Jackson, bullhead and horn sharks

These are bottom-dwelling sharks that live by crushing molluscs. Their heads are large and squarish, with distinctive crests over their eyes, and with short, pig-like snouts. There are five gill slits on each side, two large dorsal fins with spines on their leading edges, and pectoral fins that can be used for walking on the seabed. The Heterodontiformes (meaning 'many different teeth') is another very ancient order, and these sharks lived in the seas some 220 million years ago. There are eight species.

Order Pristiophoriformes

One family: Pristiophoridae

Species: Sawsharks

With their slightly flattened bodies, and mouths on the underside, sawsharks are so well adapted to life on the seabed that they resemble skates and rays more than most other sharks. Their most outstanding feature is an elongated snout equipped

with a flat blade, with teeth that are alternately large and small (not unlike the 'saw' of sawfish, although the teeth of these distantly related rays are all the same size). There are five or six gill slits on each side (depending on the species), long barbels protruding from the snout and two large dorsal fins without spines. All five species are primarily tropical, from the Indo-Pacific.

Order Squaliformes

Four families: Echinorhinidae, Squalidae, Scymnorhinidae and Oxynotidae

Species: Dogfish, Greenland and cookie-cutter sharks and spiny dogfish

There are some extraordinary sharks in this group, none more so than the Greenland shark, which is the biggest fish in the Arctic (it grows to at least 6 m (20 feet) long) and is unbelievably sluggish. The cookie-cutter shark is also very curious: it lives in deep water, has a luminescent belly and bites chunks from whales and other large vertebrates. Members of this group have a roughly cylindrical body, a short snout, five gill slits on each side, nictitating eyelids (tough third eyelids that cover the eyes completely in dangerous situations) and two dorsal fins (often with spines). There are about 80 species altogether.

Opposite, far left: The ancient sixgill shark really does have six gills on each side (most other sharks have only five). Middle: Bull sharks like shallow waters, and will enter depths of less than 1 m (39 inches). Left: The flattened body of this Pacific angel shark makes it look superficially like a ray.

Order Squatiniformes

One family: Squatinidae

Species: Angel sharks and monkfish

These bottom-dwelling sharks have flattened bodies and superficially resemble rays. They have several ray-like features, and may represent an evolutionary link between sharks and rays, but are classified as sharks. Unlike rays, their broad pectoral fins are not fused to the head or the posterior part of the body. Also, they swim like sharks rather than rays, using sideways sweeps of the tail instead of 'flying' under water with their pectoral fins. The mouth is at the front and there are five gill slits on each side and two small dorsal fins without spines. Angel sharks and monkfish live in temperate coastal waters, and there are about 13 species altogether.

Order Orectolobiformes

Seven families: Parascylliidae, Brachaeluridae, Orectolobidae, Hemiscylliidae, Stegostomatidae, Ginglymostomatidae and Rhincodontidae

Species: Known collectively as carpet sharks, although the group also includes zebra, leopard, wobbegong, nurse and whale sharks. With the obvious exception of the whale shark, the largest of all the sharks and the largest fish in the sea, the species in this order are predominantly bottom-dwelling creatures and spend much of their time lying on the seabed or swimming slowly over it. They have squarish or flattened heads, with the mouth well in front, and barbels (fleshy, whisker-like structures probably used to feel around in the sediment for prey) on the inside edges of the nostrils. There are five gill slits on each side and two dorsal fins without spines. There are just over 30 species altogether.

Opposite: This human diver is dwarfed by a harmless whale shark, the largest fish in the sea and capable of growing to a length of 12.1 m (40 feet).

Order Lamniformes

Seven families: Odontaspididae, Mitsukurinidae, Pseudocarchariidae, Megachasmidae, Alopiidae, Cetorhinidae and Lamnidae

Species: Collectively known as mackerel sharks, this diverse group includes sand tiger, megamouth, thresher, basking, great white, shortfin mako, crocodile and goblin sharks. There are 16 species altogether. These sharks tend to have a long snout, with a mouth that stretches behind the eyes (which have no nictitating eyelids). There are five gill slits on each side and two dorsal fins.

Order Carcharhiniformes

Eight families: Scyliorhinidae, Proscylliidae, Pseudotriakidae, Leptochariidae, Triakidae, Hemigaleidae, Sphyrnidae and Carcharhinidae

Species: Collectively known as ground sharks (although the Carcharhinidae family are usually known as requiem sharks). This is a very large and varied group, with more than 200 species in eight different families. The order includes many familiar species, including bronze whaler, leopard, reef, tiger, blacktip, silvertip, spinner, silky, bull, Galápagos, blue and lemon sharks and all the hammerheads. Most are streamlined hunters of open water, and some often swim with their dorsal fin breaking the surface. They have a long mouth stretching behind the eyes (which have nictitating eyelids), five gill slits on each side, and two dorsal fins without spines.

Sharks may be the most maligned, misunderstood and feared creatures on the planet – but they are also beautiful, awe-inspiring and mysterious. The more we learn about them, the harder it is not to be impressed by their supreme adaptation to the underwater world and to appreciate that the reality of their lives and habits is almost the exact opposite of all those perpetuated myths.

When did sharks first evolve?

What does palaeontology tell us about ancient sharks?

When was the 'Golden Age' of sharks?

Why did early sharks disappear?

How have sharks changed since the early days?

What methods of adaptation did sharks develop?

Which species preferred fresh water?

What happened to sharks during the Jurassic era?

Which shark was the largest species ever?

Have any ancient species survived to the present day?

Origins and Ancestors
Shark Evolution Through the Ages

Sharks in one form or another have inhabited our seas and oceans for more than 400 million years. When they first began their swim up the evolutionary ladder, Earth looked nothing like it does today: the continents had yet to break away from the ancient landmass of Pangaea, and most of the planet's surface was covered in warm seas. While sharks were beginning to inhabit that prehistoric marine world, trees were just starting their race for the sky, and dinosaurs were aeons away. By the time mammals returned to the sea, sharks were highly evolved and near-perfect predators.

Sharks witnessed the rise of our own species – the earliest origins of our hominid ancestors date back less than 4 million years, and modern humans have been around for no more than a few hundred thousand years – and may survive long enough to witness our downfall, too.

This long evolutionary history can give the false impression that sharks are primitive animals. They are often – rather derisively – called 'living fossils'. But the truth is that sharks have never stopped evolving. Nature came up with a good fundamental design at a very early stage and, for most of the millions of years since, there has been little need to change it significantly. Nevertheless, many of the earliest sharks were considerably different from modern forms; some were quite bizarre, and others

had to cope with some of the most devastating periods in the history of the world – such incredibly difficult times that most other species disappeared altogether. Modern sharks are still evolving today: they are just doing it quite slowly.

Perhaps their *coup de grâce* was to incorporate cartilage as a specialized and ingenious variation of the traditional bony skeleton. In one sweep of an evolutionary arm, they gained a light, tough structure that – unlike brittle bone – bends, mends and continues to grow throughout life. It clearly worked, or at least it seems to have contributed enormously to their survival. Unfortunately, though, this cartilage skeleton has made it incredibly difficult for palaeontologists to delve into their mysterious past.

Studying ancient sharks

The origin of modern sharks is poorly known compared with that of most other animals. Their ancestors are difficult to study because shark palaeontologists have relatively few fossil records to examine. Those ingenious cartilaginous skeletons have proved to be a major problem for researchers because, unlike bone, which fossilizes readily, cartilage tends to disintegrate soon after the sharks have died. This means that little evidence of their existence is left.

A small number of skeletons have been preserved by exceptional circumstances, and they offer a fascinating insight into the form and habits of ancient species. The discovery of perfect impressions of sharks in outcrops of Cleveland Shale (a type of soft rock from the Devonian period) along the Rocky River, near Cleveland, Ohio, in the USA, has helped enormously. These ancient creatures – which would have been instantly recognizable as sharks – were discovered in limestone rocks about 375 million years old, and lived at a time when North America was covered by water. Some of the specimens are so detailed that it has been possible to identify the contents of their stomachs, and one particular shark was so perfectly preserved that its liver and kidneys were still intact.

For the most part, however, the evolutionary history of sharks has to be pieced together mainly from fossilized teeth, with tiny scales, a few spines and calcified vertebrae adding a smattering of extra clues. It is like working on an enormously complicated jigsaw puzzle, with most of the pieces missing, or like working out what a whole person must have looked like from a couple of teeth and a fingernail.

Page 20: A whorl of fossil teeth on the lower jaw of an extinct shark called *Helicoprion,* some 300 million years old.
Opposite: The scalloped hammerhead's extraordinary head structure, known as the cephalofoil, probably evolved to serve several different functions.
Top right: The fossil tooth of an extinct megalodon is many times larger than the tooth of a modern great white shark.

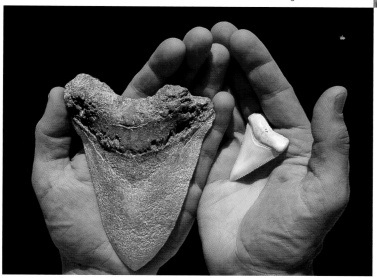

Fossilized teeth

Sharks produce prodigious numbers of teeth, and they fossilize readily, so fossil teeth are very common. They have been found everywhere from beaches to mountain-tops and from the Antarctic to the deepest part of the ocean. In the old days, they were believed to be the teeth of dragons or other monsters, and for centuries people have used them as traditional charms and decorations. For scientists they provide the only record of the existence of some extinct species; in fact, quite a few ancient sharks are known only from a single tooth.

Studying prehistoric sharks through their teeth can be both challenging and frustrating for several reasons. First, fossilized teeth provide relatively few clues about the rest of the shark. It is possible to infer something about their original owners by their size and shape, but this requires a lot of informed guesswork. If the teeth are long and pointed, for example, they might have been used for grabbing soft-bodied, elusive prey, which would suggest a shark that was probably a fast, aggressive swimmer. If the teeth are much flatter and more peg-like, their owner was probably a bottom-feeder specializing in hard-bodied but slow-moving prey. Shark palaeontologists have to be careful about drawing too many firm conclusions, though, because some sharks have different teeth in different parts of the jaw, and these may vary between males and females.

The study of fossilized shark teeth was further complicated by the recent discovery that some baby sharks shed and replace their teeth while still inside the womb. These baby teeth can be quite different in shape from those of the adults, and the fear is that some fossilized embryonic teeth may have been mistakenly identified as belonging to different species altogether. The embryonic teeth of a great white shark, for example, look almost identical to the adult teeth of a sand tiger shark – and they are in completely different families.

Early sharks

Primitive fishes probably began to appear for the first time about half a billion years ago. The earliest complete fossil, which was discovered in Australia in rocks 480 million years old, belonged to a bony fish without jaws that is believed to have lived in coastal waters.

The first sharks may have appeared soon afterwards – at least, soon afterwards in geological terms. We know virtually nothing about them because the only clues to their existence are tiny scales found in deposits some 450 million years old. But these are so similar to the scales of later sharks that there is little

doubt they came from sharks of one kind or another. It may be that the sharks evolved before their teeth, which would explain why no teeth from this time have been found.

Some of the first fishes with jaws belonged to an ancient group known as the acanthodians, or spiny sharks, which appeared during the Silurian period (438–408 million years ago). Some of them survived right through until the early Permian, some 280 million years ago. These were not true sharks, and probably not even the ancestors of true sharks, but they were certainly spiny and had vaguely shark-like bodies. They had rows of sharp teeth to feast on their jawless cousins, and were generally quite small – less than 20 cm (8 inches) long.

The oldest fossil shark teeth found so far are from the Early Devonian, and are estimated to be around 400 million years old. Their owners were probably no more than 30 cm (12 inches) long (the teeth themselves are tiny – no more than 4 mm (0.16 inches) across) but no fossilized skeletons have been found, so we can only speculate about their appearance. A possible close relative, believed to have lived around 380 million years ago, was

Below and opposite, left to right: Acanthodian (shark-like but not a true shark), *Helicoprion* (with its elaborate spiral of teeth), *Stethacanthus* (one of the strangest-looking early sharks) and *Cladoselache* (one of the best-known early sharks).

Antarctilamna. As its name suggests, this species was first discovered in Antarctica, and it is known from the oldest shark fossil consisting of more than teeth and scales. Just 40 cm (16 inches) long, and distinctly shark-like, it had a spine in front of its dorsal fin and cusped teeth (with pointed elevations).

Intact skeletons, skin and even muscles have been found of a shark called *Cladoselache*, which is one of the best-known early sharks and shares many of the features of modern sharks. *Cladoselache* is known from remains in the Cleveland Shale in the USA, and seems to have been the predominant shark of that era. It probably grew to about 2 m (6 feet) in length and had a slender and streamlined, torpedo-shaped body. It had two dorsal fins roughly equal in size, each with a stout spine in front, as well as pectoral fins and five pairs of gill slits. Perhaps the most interesting feature of *Cladoselache* was its caudal (tail) fin because the upper and lower lobes were equal in size, suggesting that it was probably a fast swimmer. *Cladoselache* was well adapted for feeding on fast-swimming fishes – and for escaping the monster fishes called placoderms that were probably major predators at the time – and was probably an inhabitant of the open ocean. But for all our knowledge about these ancient fish, it is unlikely that *Cladoselache* is the much sought-after ancestor of modern sharks, primarily because it did not have claspers (the distinctive sexual organs found in all male sharks today).

Diversification

All fishes, including sharks, diversified greatly at around the time of *Cladoselache*. This extraordinary period, which began 330 million years ago, has been dubbed the 'Age of Fishes' and represents the first major radiation of sharks. The so-called 'Golden Age of Sharks' was around the same time – a period of great diversification and proliferation, which produced some very strange-looking species.

Perhaps the weirdest-looking shark alive at the time was *Stethacanthus*. An almost complete specimen was unearthed next to a housing estate in, of all places, the suburbs of Glasgow in Scotland. The top of its blunt head was covered with a helmet of small teeth and, instead of an anterior dorsal fin, it had an awkward, mushroom-like structure sticking out of its back, with dozens more hook-shaped teeth on top. No one knows what this unlikely structure – often described as resembling a shaving brush or hairbrush – was used for. It may have been for anchoring *Stethacanthus* to the underside of larger fish, like a modern remora; it could have played a role in courtship (although it was present in both males and females); or it may have been used in defence or, by looking vaguely like a mouth, to frighten off predators.

Another strange-looking shark from the beginning of the Carboniferous was one called *Helicoprion*. The teeth on its lower jaw formed a tight, elaborate spiral, about 20 cm (8 inches) in

diameter, dropping away under the apex of the jaw and then back into a cavity underneath. Again, the purpose of this bizarre contraption is a mystery. However, it might have been a precursor to the rotating rows of teeth in the jaws of modern sharks – one theory is that a spiral formed as old teeth were rotated to make way for new teeth. No *Helicoprion* carcasses have ever been found, and the only evidence for its existence is these fossilized teeth.

Equally bizarre is the unicorn shark or *Falcatus*, which had an L-shaped 'horn' growing out of its back and over the top of its head. A pair of unicorn sharks 8–10 cm (3–4 inches) long was found joined together, with one grabbing the horn of the other in its mouth, in Carboniferous deposits from 360 million years ago at Bear Gulch in Montana, USA. This suggests that the horn may have had a role to play in courtship, perhaps providing something to grip during mating.

The rapid diversification of sharks came to an end in the late Carboniferous period, about 290 million years ago. Then, at the end of the Permian period some 245 million years ago, the world faced the greatest mass extinction of all time. Climatic conditions began to change dramatically: the North and South Poles cooled, water levels dropped and volcanic activity intensified. These rapid and extraordinary changes killed off about 96 per cent of all marine life. Most shark species joined the casualty list, but some survived by moving into fresh water, and others simply managed

to adapt because they were fast enough to pursue prey in the open ocean and cunning enough to scour the ocean floor for molluscs and crustaceans.

Survival of the fittest

Two main shark groups began to fill the ecological niches vacated by so many extinct species. The first included the xenacanth sharks, which were the ones that moved into fresh water. One species, more like a modern conger eel than a shark, was *Xenacanthus*. Some 75 cm (30 inches) long, it had an extended dorsal fin that stretched all the way down its back and around its tail to blend in with an unusual double anal fin. But its most distinctive feature was a single spine, probably used for defence, which grew backwards out of the top of its head.

The hybodonts formed the second surviving group, and most of these sharks remained in the sea. They were not the immediate ancestors of modern sharks, but resembled them in basic body structure and way of life. They were unspecialized and even possessed two types of teeth – pointed ones at the front, for grasping, and broader ones at the back, for crushing. This enabled them to vary their feeding habits according to the food available at the time. Unlike modern sharks (but like modern chimaeras, which are distant relatives), the males had hooks on their heads, which were probably used to grasp the females during mating. Most significant of all, the males had copulatory organs in the form of claspers attached to their pelvic fins.

We do not know why the ancient hybodonts and xenacanths disappeared (around the same time as the dinosaurs). It might have been intense competition from carnivorous, fish-shaped reptiles. But what we do know is that modern sharks were developing before they became extinct, and ultimately replaced them. The first of these modern sharks probably appeared a little over 200 million years ago, around the beginning of the Jurassic period. These newcomers had streamlined bodies, five pairs of external gill slits, two well-developed dorsal fins, pectoral and pelvic fins, and a powerful vertical tail. They also had more flexible jaws that could be thrust forwards when feeding.

Most of the shark families in existence today are believed to have evolved within the past 140 million years. Streamlined, fast-swimming and equipped with their remarkable assortment of senses, these near-perfect predators must have made formidable

Below and opposite, left to right: Megalodon (the largest shark ever to have lived), *Xenacanthus* (an early freshwater shark), Hybodont (resembling the ancestors of modern sharks) and *Falcatus* (otherwise known as the unicorn shark).

competitors for sea-living relatives of the dinosaurs, such as the long-necked plesiosaurs and the shark-like ichthyosaurs, and they have held their position at the top of the food chain ever since.

Megalodon

One of the most intriguing of all the ancient sharks is the megatooth, or megalodon. This was the largest shark ever to have lived, and one of the most formidable predators ever to stalk the planet. It is a close relative of the great white shark (which looks tiny in comparison), and was a monster predator at the top of the food chain from a little more than 20 million years ago.

There has been much debate about the maximum length of megalodon, and for many years it was believed that it could grow to 37 m (120 feet) or more. There is a famous photograph showing four scientists standing and two kneeling inside an inaccurate model of the giant jaws of a megalodon. The size of the model had been based on the largest discovered teeth, but if the scientists had used a full set of the varied teeth discovered (more likely to have occurred naturally), it would have been about one third smaller. Nevertheless, megalodon did grow to an impressive size – probably reaching a length of at least 15 m (50 feet) and a

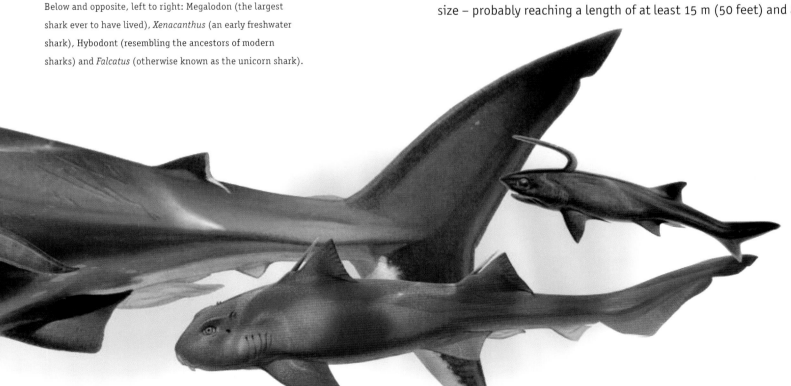

weight of 25–50 tonnes (28–56 tons) – and was many times larger than *Tyrannosaurus rex*. It is believed to have had a mouth gape of about 2 m (6 feet). Its scientific name means 'the shark with big teeth', and, indeed, its razor-sharp, arrow-shaped teeth were up to 18 cm (7 inches) long – more than three times longer than those of present-day great white sharks. It is uncertain whether megalodon was an ancestor of the great white, or whether it represents an evolutionary dead end.

It probably lived in the coastal regions of warm seas (its fossils are commonly found in near-shore deposits) and is likely to have fed on whales and dolphins. The great whales, in particular, would have been good to eat and could possibly have been killed by these huge, powerful sharks.

Megalodon probably became extinct around 2 million years ago, although some shark enthusiasts believe that it might have survived as recently as 12,000 years ago. A few people, against most scientific evidence, still hold out hope that it continues to lurk in the ocean depths. Megalodon teeth have been dredged from the seabed in both the Atlantic and the Pacific, suggesting that they may have been deposited quite recently (older teeth would have been covered by so much silt that the dredging gear could not have reached them). However, assuming that it *is* extinct, the reason for its disappearance is still a mystery. One possibility is that some whales started to migrate towards the poles to feed during the summer (perhaps to avoid predation by these large sharks) and, sure enough, megalodon was ill-equipped to follow them into such icy waters.

Living fossils

Some of the most extraordinary sharks living today probably deserve to be called 'living fossils' because they are surprisingly similar in appearance to sharks that swam in the ancient seas more than 100 million years ago. Although they are rarely seen, because they tend to live hidden away in the dark ocean depths, they provide palaeontologists with an intriguing window on the prehistoric world.

One particular living fossil with an extraordinary story is the goblin shark, which has a long, flat, dagger-like snout that has earned it a rather unfair reputation as the world's ugliest shark. It was discovered in 1898 by an amateur naturalist, who had spent the day rummaging through the catch at a fish market in Yokohama, Japan. The specimen was a 1.06-m (42-inch) juvenile male with protruding jaws, needle-sharp teeth, small beady eyes and a flabby body. It had been caught in a region of very deep water called the Black Current. Soon after it was officially declared a new species, experts realized that the goblin shark had already been examined by the scientific community – as a fossil shark named *Scapanorhynchus* (meaning 'shovel-nose'). Until that remarkable find in Japan, the species had been thought to have been extinct for over 100 million years.

Now officially called *Mitsukurina owstoni*, the goblin shark seems to have changed little over the millennia. It is found in deep water – the tooth of one individual was discovered in a submarine cable at a depth of 1400 m (4593 feet) – and we now know that it is widely distributed in many parts of the world. It grows to a length of at least 4.3 m (14 feet) and, when it is brought up to the surface, is pinkish-grey in colour with darker fins. Its skin is very unusual: sandpaper-like in texture, rubbery in consistency and translucent. Very little is known about the life and habits of this deep-living and fierce-looking shark. Its curious snout, in particular, is a source of much debate. The shape suggests that it could serve as a tool for flushing out small fish and other prey from inside crevices, but it is probably too soft and rubbery to be used in this way. However, there is one interesting clue: it is covered with a bountiful supply of electro-receptors, so is more likely to be used for detecting prey in the dark depths of the ocean.

The frilled or eel shark is very like *Cladoselache* in appearance, and probably the least shark-like of all modern sharks. There is considerable debate about its evolution: one theory is that it is a direct descendant of *Cladoselache*, but another is that the similarities are simply the result of convergent evolution. Shaped more like an eel, with six large, frilly gill slits, its mouth is at the front of its head and its nostrils are on top (both are on the underside in present-day sharks). Its eyes are large, suggesting that it is a deep-water species, and its lateral line system (used for sensing vibrations and movements in the water) is an open groove rather than a tube partly buried in the skin. It is widely distributed, but poorly known because it usually lives at depths of 100–1300 m (330–4260 feet). The frilled shark probably chases prey among the rocky reefs and ledges on the steep drop-offs along continental shelves.

The frilled shark's jaws and teeth resemble fossil specimens from 350 million years ago, but the fact that it has six gill slits is particularly interesting. Most modern sharks have just five gill slits. The frilled shark belongs to the ancient order Hexanchiformes, which includes the sixgill and sevengill sharks. They also live in deep water and, as their name suggests, have six or seven gill slits on each side. Their jaws and vertebrae resemble fossil counterparts from 190 million years ago.

It is surprising how much information has been accumulated over many years of work, but shark palaeontology is a difficult and painstaking science. Not surprisingly, most experts believe that the vast majority of prehistoric sharks – perhaps even some living fossils – have probably escaped our attention altogether. We have no clues that they ever existed. Even the prehistoric species that are known to science still hold many secrets, and researchers have not been able to piece together a seamless narrative showing how one species has evolved from other, earlier ones. There are so many gaps in our knowledge that new discoveries (through fossil evidence and, more recently, genetic analysis) are constantly throwing old theories into doubt. But it is a fascinating field of research with plenty more surprises and revelations virtually guaranteed.

Opposite: Scientists standing inside an inaccurate model of the jaws of an extinct megalodon (the correct size would have been about one third smaller – albeit still impressive).
Left: The poorly known goblin shark has an elongated snout flattened into the shape of a paddle.

What determines the shape of a shark's body?

How important is coloration?

What is neutral buoyancy?

Are there different ways of controlling buoyancy?

How do sharks swim?

Why do sharks have several different types of fin?

Is shark skin effective as armour?

How do sharks breathe?

What's the difference between warm-blooded and cold-blooded sharks?

Just how clever are sharks?

The Perfect Body
Biology Surpasses Technology

Sharks may have a long evolutionary history, and still retain anatomical features that are millions of years old, but a team of the world's top aeronautical engineers and naval architects equipped with the best computer technology available probably could not improve on their perfectly designed bodies. Whether functioning as supremely streamlined swimming machines, able to outpace most other fish in the sea with the merest flick of their tails, or whether lurking on or near the seabed, ready to ambush passing prey with a lightning strike, they could not be better prepared.

Everything, from their overall shape to the surface of their skin, is 'technologically advanced'. Sharks have the best-shaped bodies, the best internal anatomy, the best swimming aids, and even the best colours for their challenging underwater world.

Living in water is a mixed blessing. On the one hand, it is a dense medium that clings like glue to anything moving through it – as anyone who has tried walking through water will know. On the other, that same density buffers the effects of gravity and provides support and buoyancy, meaning that sharks and other water-dwellers do not have to use as much energy as land-dwellers merely to stay upright and in one place. Sharks are designed to take full advantage of these benefits and, of course, to overcome the difficulties of living in water.

Shape and colour

The shape of a shark's body depends on the kind of life it leads. Fast swimmers, such as great whites and silky sharks, have torpedo-shaped bodies and powerful tails designed to cut through the water at great speed. The diameter of their bodies is greatest at about a third of the way back from the snout, and it tapers away from there towards the front and back; this shape lets water flow smoothly over the body and reduces turbulence. Even the head is cone-shaped, or flattened, to make movement through the water as efficient as possible. The result is impressive: the shortfin mako, for example, is a biological torpedo capable of bursts of speed estimated to be as much as 75 km/h (46 mph). Its streamlined body and missile-like nose cone provide the ultimate

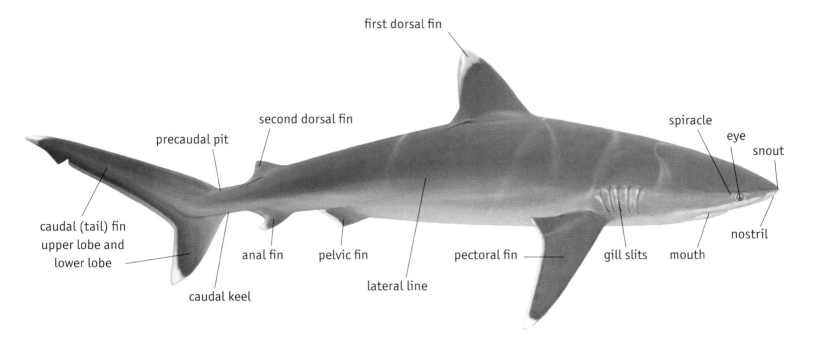

first dorsal fin

second dorsal fin

precaudal pit

spiracle

eye

snout

caudal (tail) fin
upper lobe and
lower lobe

anal fin

pelvic fin

pectoral fin

gill slits

mouth

nostril

caudal keel

lateral line

biological example of hydrodynamic efficiency and power. The pectoral fins are short, to reduce drag, and stiff, to manoeuvre at high speed; and the claspers of the male are retracted into special grooves behind the pelvic fins.

Sharks designed to feed on or near the seabed, such as smallspotted catsharks, tend to be sluggish and have little need of streamlining and athletic prowess. Many of them are content to stay in one place (they often end up dying close to where they were born) because they get all the food they need without having to travel much at all. Their aim is to avoid being seen, so they rely more on camouflage and concealment than speed. They have more flexible, and often flattened, ray-like bodies that are better suited to being buried in the sandy bottom or hiding in crevices among rocks and corals waiting to ambush their prey.

Page 30: Oceanic whitetip sharks showing off their
distinctively long, paddle-shaped pectoral fins.
Above: The external features of a typical shark.
Opposite: The silky shark is named after the smooth,
silky texture of its skin.

Between these two extremes – the fast swimmers and the sluggish hiders – sharks come in a variety of different shapes based on the same basic theme.

Even the coloration of sharks is an important design feature. Bony fishes are often very brightly coloured – some are even iridescent – and they use their colours in extravagant courtship displays to attract mates. But sharks use colour for something completely different: camouflage. Few sharks are brightly coloured because they are more intent on being able to hide from their predators and sneak up on their prey. They have evolved a form of coloration called counter-shading, which is a distinguishing feature of many sharks. Basically, they are dark above (usually grey or brown) and light below (usually lighter grey, lighter brown or white). This makes them difficult to spot from above, against the dark ocean depths, and equally difficult to spot from underneath, against the light ocean surface.

There are many variations, and some exceptions, to this basic counter-shaded colour scheme. The Pacific angel shark, spotted wobbegong and other species that live on the seabed are

sharks are an exception – they have no bone at all, and their entire skeleton is made of cartilage.

These cartilaginous skeletons, or, more precisely, the specific patterns in which they are calcified, are the most defining characteristic of sharks. They are simpler than the skeletons of most bony fish and consist of basic cartilage supports for the back, fins and gills. The cartilage is more flexible than bone, enabling sharks to turn around in a smaller space than bony fishes, yet it is still tough and provides protection and support for the internal body organs (portions of the skeleton that experience extreme physical stress, such as vertebrae, parts of the skull and jaws, are stiffened by extra calcification). Cartilage also keeps growing as long as the shark lives. But its main advantage is its light weight. Whereas bone is twice as dense as water, cartilage is only slightly denser. This is a major factor in enabling sharks to maintain a degree of neutral buoyancy – the ability to 'hover' in the water without sinking or floating up to the surface. A cartilaginous skeleton is so fundamental to modern sharks that it is unlikely they would be capable of such agile movement had they evolved bony skeletons.

masters of disguise and superbly camouflaged to blend in with the sand, mud and rocks on the seabed. Some even have frilly bits on their heads that look remarkably like seaweed. The whale shark is another good example: it has an intriguing mixture of light-coloured spots, bands and stripes which, depending on the theory you believe, could resemble a school of fish or even the dappled sunlight on a shallow coral reef.

Beyond their basic streamlined shape and counter-shaded coloration, sharks have incorporated a wide range of other design features to achieve near-perfect bodies. Among other adaptations, they have special skeletons, impressive armour plating that reduces drag, and even internal flotation devices.

Cartilaginous skeleton

In the early stages of development most fish, amphibians, reptiles, birds and mammals have cartilage – an elastic, fibrous connective tissue – instead of bone. But as development progresses, and the foetus grows, most of this cartilage is replaced by bone (we retain small amounts of cartilage throughout life in our nose, ears, trachea, larynx and joints). Just like most other vertebrates, the vast majority of adult fishes have hard, dense skeletons made of bones composed of calcium, but

Oil-filled liver

Bony fishes control buoyancy in the water by using a sac-like extension of the gut, called the swim bladder, which acts like an internal lifebuoy. This can be inflated or deflated according to their depth to keep them perfectly positioned in the water without having to expend unnecessary energy by swimming. There is, however, a price to pay for this facility. First, the fishes' control must be precise, since depth and water pressure affect

Above: The spotted wobbegong uses camouflage to blend in with its surroundings.
Opposite: A thresher shark leaps high into the air to reveal its enormous, scythe-like tail.

the size of the swim bladder. More importantly, adding or removing the gas in a swim bladder is quite a slow process: bubbles of gas are picked up and dropped off by the blood, so if the fish rises to the surface too quickly, the volume of air in the bladder expands with the decreasing pressure, making the bladder likely to burst.

Sharks do not have a swim bladder, and this enables them to move up and down the water column very quickly without any risk. But they still need help in maintaining neutral buoyancy. Even though they have low-density cartilaginous skeletons and their bodies are hydrodynamically efficient to provide lift, their body tissues are denser than water, so the natural tendency is for them to sink, albeit slowly. They use their enormous oil-filled livers as flotation devices instead. Bony fishes have relatively small livers, but a shark's liver can account for as much as 25 per cent of its total body weight. This is certainly true in the basking shark, which has a gigantic twin-lobed liver that runs the entire length of its abdominal cavity. The liver in all sharks contains a fatty substance called squalene, and this accounts for as much as 90 per cent of the liver weight in some species. Squalene is much less dense than water (only 0.86, compared with sea water at 1.026 and the rest of the shark's body at about 1.10), so it dramatically reduces the overall weight of the shark under water. The liver therefore helps to keep the shark afloat.

An exception to this method of flotation is the sand tiger shark, which may be on its evolutionary journey to developing its own bony-fish-like swim bladder. It goes to the surface to swallow air, then holds it inside the upper portion of its stomach, where the lining is thinner and there are fewer digestive juices than lower down. This enables it to remain motionless in the water without expending energy on swimming, and without sinking.

Shark fins and swimming

Even with a cartilaginous skeleton and an enormous oil-filled liver, most sharks are still heavier than water (some deep-water sharks have enough liver oil to achieve perfect neutral buoyancy, but they are the exception). If most sharks were ever to stop swimming, they would slowly sink into the abyss. So they make the swimming easier, and help to counteract their negative buoyancy, by having pectoral fins and tails that are shaped like aeroplane wings and provide a natural upward lift. In hammerheads and some other species the heads also create lift. In addition, they may take advantage of warm, rising ocean currents to be carried up the water column, just like birds using thermals to rise in the air.

Sharks swim by moving their head from side to side. This sends a wave down the length of the body, which gets progressively greater towards the tail. As the body and the tail swing outwards and backwards in an S-shaped curve, pushing against the water, the shark moves forwards. Sharks are incredibly efficient swimmers, but they do not move with quite the same grace or mobility as many bony fishes, mainly because they do not have as many movable parts. They can swerve, but they cannot swim backwards, for example.

They have as many as five different types of fin: three types that are unpaired (dorsal, anal and caudal) and two that are paired (pectoral and pelvic). Each type probably performs several

Opposite: Shark skin viewed under an electron microscope (110 times magnification).

different functions: the paired pectoral fins, for example, which are located on the lower sides, behind the head and close to the gill slits, provide lift when the shark is moving up and down in the water column, provide stability when it is travelling at a constant depth, and are essential for steering and turning. They are like an aeroplane's wings, and together with the pelvic fins provide lift when the shark swims forwards. In cross-section, the leading edge is slightly thicker than the trailing edge. This shape works just as it does on a wing: a partial vacuum forms on the upper surface and this causes a slight pressure to push up on the underside, which is sufficient to pull the fin (and the shark) upwards. There are usually two dorsal fins on the shark's back (the first one, farthest from the tail, is often much larger than the second), and these provide lateral stability, preventing the shark from yawing or deviating from its straight-line course, rather like the keel of a sailing boat. It is the first dorsal fin, slicing through the surface of the water, that says 'shark' in so many horror and adventure movies. The paired pelvic fins are located underneath the shark, roughly between the first dorsal fin and the tail, and help to provide natural lift and control movement. Behind them, also on the underside, is the single anal fin for yet more stability.

There is also a caudal (tail) fin, which produces forward thrust. It varies enormously in size and shape from species to species, depending on their lifestyle. Sharks with tails that have an almost equal upper and lower lobe, such as the shortfin mako and great white, tend to be fast-swimming; their tails look remarkably similar to those of other fast swimmers, such as sailfish and swordfish. Some species, such as the tiger shark, have a tail with a longer upper lobe. Although there is considerable debate about the way this design works, it is found in open-ocean hunters and is probably an adaptation for cruising. Slow-

swimming bottom-dwellers have large, flat tails, or tails with very large upper lobes (some retain a powerful tail for long-distance movement across the seabed). In some sharks the spinal column has a kink that turns upward into the tail's upper lobe; in others, it is straight and the tail is kinked down slightly to fit on to it.

The most impressive caudal fins are the scythe-shaped tails of thresher sharks. It is the upper lobe of the tail that is exceptionally long, perhaps equalling the length of the rest of the body. Given that the common thresher may be able to grow up to 6.1 m (20 feet) long, its tail length could be as much as 3 m (10 feet). It is believed to be used as a weapon, like a whip, to herd or stun prey animals, such as fishes and squid. The sharks swim around a shoal in ever-decreasing circles and lash out to herd their prey together. Then they rush in, swatting and swiping, before turning back to swallow their stunned or dead victims. There is little direct evidence to support this intriguing theory, but in some parts of the world killer whales use a similar technique, and sea anglers have reported catching thresher sharks on live baits – not hooked in the mouth, but in the tail.

Shark fins are surprisingly different from those in bony fishes. They are not the thin, flexible fins supported by delicate spines that are found in most bony fishes, but are thick and stiffened by cartilaginous rods and internal fibres of collagen. They are all fixed in shape, and the vertical, unpaired fins have a fixed angle too. This makes sharks less manoeuvrable in the water, and less capable of fine control, than most bony fishes.

Shark skin

Shark skin feels smooth if stroked from front to back, but is so rough when stroked from back to front that it can scrape human skin raw. Some small fish actually rub themselves against shark skin to remove their own external parasites. As well as providing an all-over covering that holds the whole shark together, the skin

greatly improves hydrodynamic efficiency and protects the shark against injury.

The skin is covered in tiny placoid scales, usually less than 1 mm (1/32 inch) across, each of which is a tooth-like dermal denticle. The denticles are rather like normal teeth, complete with an outer covering of hard enamel around a dentine layer and pulp cavity, and normally face backwards. Each species has denticles of a different shape and they are uniquely shaped on different parts of the body – more rounded on the snout, for example, and pointed on the back.

The dermal denticles help to improve hydrodynamic efficiency by breaking up the interface between skin and water, thus reducing turbulence when the shark is swimming; the enamel crowns have multiple sharp ridges and grooves that reduce drag. Experiments during the 1980s at Scripps Institution of Oceanography in California demonstrated that, weight for weight, a blue shark was so much more hydrodynamically efficient than a submarine that it required six times less driving power. In fact, shark skin is so effective that engineers are now attempting to replicate dermal denticles to reduce turbulence in aircraft, submarines, racing yachts and even bathing suits – experimenting with rough rather than smooth surfaces for their products. The results in terms of energy saving are already proving to be remarkable.

The dermal denticles also form an impressive outer layer of armour, like prickly chain-mail. The skin on the upper side of a whale shark is so thick – up to 10 cm (4 inches) – and impenetrable that harpoons and rifle bullets fired at close range have been known to bounce off its back.

The scales in bony fishes are essentially smooth, overlapping bony plates, and they grow as the fish grows larger. But this is not the case in sharks. The denticles stay the same size throughout the shark's life, but as it grows, more of them are added to fill in the 'gaps', and old ones are quickly replaced by new ones.

Breathing under water

Like all animals, sharks have to breathe. Just as we rely on gaseous oxygen in air, they depend on dissolved oxygen in water.

Sharks breathe by taking water in through their mouths and passing it over their gills (which, effectively, are their 'lungs'), where oxygen is extracted. Sharks that swim fast in the open ocean usually swim with their mouths slightly open so that oxygen-rich sea water flows in naturally and is forced over their gills and out through the gill slits as they speed along. The technical term for this is ram-jet ventilation. The popular perception that sharks must keep swimming in order to breathe is partly true, but only for some species under certain conditions. Highly mobile species, such as shortfin makos, oceanic whitetips and blue sharks, rely on this system almost exclusively, and must be constantly in motion if they want to keep breathing. They suffocate fairly quickly if brought to a stop in a fishing net, for example. Other species, however, do not have to keep swimming.

Bull sharks, lemon sharks, whitetip reef sharks and many other species can actively pump water over their gills by opening and closing their mouths, and some bottom-dwellers, such as tasselled wobbegongs and Pacific angel sharks, do this as a matter of course. They open their mouths, expand the walls of their pharynx to suck in water, then close their mouths and raise the floor to propel the water over their gills and out through their gill slits. The muscles they use to perform this task collectively form what is known as the gill pump. There are valves to stop water going down the throat and special flaps prevent it from coming in through the gill slits. The Port Jackson shark has a modified version of the gill pump, designed to pump water in through the first pair of gill slits and out over the remaining four.

Most bottom-dwelling sharks have an alternative method for taking in water to absorb oxygen. They have two large holes just behind the eyes – one on each side of the head – called spiracles. These holes serve as auxiliary water inlets when the animal is feeding or resting on the seabed. If they were to use their mouths, which lie very close to the seabed, they could choke their gills with debris or sand particles stirred up from the bottom. Without spiracles, they would find it hard or even impossible to breathe. Skates and rays use a similar system. In most other species, the spiracles are barely visible and serve no known purpose, or they are absent altogether. An interesting exception is the whale shark, which has very large spiracles that are used as hiding places by its accompanying community of small fishes. Whale sharks and basking sharks use their massive gills for breathing, but they also use them as plankton-filters for feeding.

Bony fishes have a single gill opening with a hard protective plate, called the operculum, on each side of the head, but most sharks have five pairs of external gill slits (some more primitive species, such as the aptly named sixgill and sevengill sharks, have more) that are clearly visible from the outside. Each arch-shaped gill is supported by a cartilage bar, which curves around the side

of the throat cavity, and carries a double fringe of hundreds of fine, feathered gill filaments. Each of the filaments is made of thousands of tiny, leaf-like branches called lamellae. The design is very similar to the inside of our own lungs, creating a huge surface area to absorb as much oxygen as possible. The lamellae contain microscopic blood vessels, called capillaries, and have incredibly thin walls so that the blood on the inside flows very close to the water on the outside.

From a separate chamber beneath the gills, the shark's heart pumps blood to the capillary beds in the gill arches. Fast-moving sharks have bigger hearts than those that move slowly: a large heart is essential to pump blood around the body fast enough. As water is pumped over the gills, carbon dioxide passes out of the blood into the water, and oxygen diffuses out of the water into the blood. From there, the oxygen is sent via the bloodstream to all the tissues and organs in the body. The efficiency of this exchange mechanism is improved enormously by a counter-current system –

Left: While hiding inside a tiny cave in its coral reef home in the Andaman Sea, a juvenile whitetip reef shark breathes by opening and closing its mouth to pump water over its gills.

water flows over the gills from front to back, while blood flows through them from back to front – which enhances the rate and efficiency of oxygen diffusion into the blood. The principle of gas exchange at the gills is quite simple: whenever the levels of oxygen or carbon dioxide are unequal inside and outside the shark, the balance must be restored by a process known as osmosis. If there is less oxygen in the blood than the surrounding water, oxygen passes into the bloodstream to correct the imbalance.

The end result is not dissimilar to our own breathing, or respiration. The shark takes water into its mouth or spiracles and over its gills (the equivalent of breathing air into the lungs) and then expels it through the gill slits (the equivalent of breathing out). It is an impressively efficient system. Sea water contains only about 1 per cent dissolved oxygen at the surface (the proportion drops to less than 0.025 per cent in deep water), and

Above: Basking sharks use their enormous gills to filter planktonic crustaceans and fish eggs out of the water, as well as to breathe.
Opposite: The shortfin mako is one of several species of sharks that are effectively warm-blooded.

shark gills can extract roughly 80 per cent of it; for comparison, fresh air contains about 21 per cent gaseous oxygen and our lungs can extract only 25 per cent of it.

Studies on epaulette sharks, so called for the black patterns resembling military insignia on their 'shoulders', reveal an extraordinary ability to survive long periods without oxygen. Epaulettes are confined to eastern Australia and Papua New Guinea, where they live in water just centimetres deep. This is isolated from the ocean at low tide; during the day, its oxygen is replenished by photosynthesizing algae, but at night oxygen

levels plummet to as low as 20 per cent of normal. This is low enough for most fish to suffer brain damage within a few minutes. Worse still, at extremely low tides, the water disappears altogether and the sharks are left high and dry, lying on the exposed reef limp and comatose. But the epaulette sharks positively thrive in this challenging environment. In captivity, they regularly survive three hours with no oxygen at all, appearing to be dead, then suddenly coming back to life. They can even recover after their tails begin to stiffen – an early sign of rigor mortis. Since they can survive oxygen deprivation at a temperature close to human body temperature (most other animals capable of surviving oxygen deprivation do it at freezing cold temperatures), scientists are studying epaulette sharks in the hope that they might be able to learn how to improve treatment of medical conditions, such as strokes and heart attacks, where organs are deprived of oxygen.

Warm-blooded sharks

Sharks in the family Lamnidae – including the shortfin mako, great white and the porbeagle – have a sophisticated modification of the circulatory system that effectively makes them homeothermic (warm-blooded). Thresher sharks have a similar system.

There is a special network of blood vessels, called the *rete mirabile* (wonderful net), which consists of layers of thick-walled arteries and thin-walled veins sandwiched between muscle. This acts as a heat-exchange system. Heat produced by muscle activity would normally be lost in the oxygen-poor blood leaving the muscle, but instead it is used to warm the cooler, oxygen-rich blood as it enters the muscle. In this way, the muscles are bathed in warm blood about 5–7°C (34–36°F) above the temperature of the surrounding sea water, and relatively little heat is lost to the outside world via the gills.

This gives the sharks a considerable advantage over their cold-blooded prey. Chemical reactions within the muscle fibres proceed at two or three times the normal rate, and this enables the sharks to remain active and react quickly even in cold water. It also enables them to dive to much colder water in the ocean depths in search of prey. And a warmer stomach – a great white shark stomach can be up to 13.7°C (41°F) above the sea temperature – results in much faster digestion, which enables the sharks to feed again rapidly, should the opportunity arise. The only problem is that the heat-exchange system uses more energy, which must be taken in as extra food.

In contrast to these homeothermic sharks, most other sharks are poikilothermic (cold-blooded). They do not have a wonderful net, and, unlike warm-blooded mammals, they do not generate heat by digesting food, but instead have a variable body temperature. Their body temperature normally matches the temperature of the surrounding sea water: if that changes, the shark's body temperature changes as well.

Salt balance

Sea water has a relatively high concentration of salts – higher than is natural inside most animals. If the salt concentration is weaker inside the shark than it is in the sea water, water is sucked out of the shark's body by osmosis (a natural process causing water to diffuse from one side to the other to restore the imbalance) and the shark could die. But sharks are able to stop this happening by maintaining an artificially high internal concentration of salts. This is achieved by retaining large quantities of the body's natural waste products, especially urea, in the blood. Some species, such as the Greenland shark, smell strongly of stale urine as a result.

Sharks also produce an organic compound, trimethylamine oxide, that helps to maintain the osmotic balance. And when excess sodium chloride enters the body after they swallow sea water or ingest prey, it is actively removed by secretions from a specialized organ called the rectal gland.

So efficient is this process of altering salinity that several species of shark, including tiger sharks, can even enter brackish water in river estuaries for feeding visits. This is impressive because the salinity of the water is changing continuously as river water mixes with sea water, so they need to alter their salt concentrations accordingly.

Perhaps most impressive of all is the bull shark, one of the few shark species that can live in fresh water. Also known as the freshwater whaler, the Zambezi shark and the Lake Nicaragua shark, it is found hundreds of kilometres up tropical rivers, especially in Africa and South America. It has to lower the urea content in its body to limit the amount of water diffusing into its body (the reverse of the problem encountered in sea water), and removes any excess water via the kidneys as very dilute urine.

Shark intelligence

One major problem with studying intelligence is the difficulty in defining the word itself. Many definitions have been proposed over the years, but in basic terms intelligence is the ability to understand. It encompasses the ability to learn from experience and thus to analyse new situations rather than simply react to them. Intelligent animals are able to *solve* problems by grasping

Opposite: Slower, bottom-dwelling sharks, such as this tawny nurse shark in Thailand, tend to have smaller brains than their more active, open-ocean relatives.

fundamental principles and by making considered judgements about the possible consequences of their actions. This is quite different from instinctive responses that get things right merely by trial and error. Clearly, considered judgement cannot be achieved in the absence of a thinking process, but whether or not it requires self-awareness or subjective thinking is another matter altogether. We are a long way from drawing any definitive conclusions if, indeed, we will ever be able to draw them.

Perhaps the greatest mistake we make is attempting to compare shark intelligence with our own. After all, we have only a human perspective and can scarcely imagine what goes on inside another animal's mind. Sharks have embarked upon an entirely different evolutionary path, and no matter how they fare in human intelligence tests, the details of their own intelligence suits their needs. They could still be more intelligent in their world than we are in ours.

Sharks tend to have relatively large brains, although brain size and complexity varies enormously from species to species. The brain to body ratio is typically around 1:1000 to 1:500, which does not compare particularly well with 1:50 in humans, but is better than in most bony fishes, and compares favourably with some birds and small mammals.

However, a large brain does not necessarily mean great intelligence. A shark's brain is relatively simple, and large portions of it are devoted to analysing the mass of information from its supersenses, particularly the sense of smell. Nearly a third of a typical shark's brain is devoted to smell. Other parts of the brain are devoted to controlling movements of the body, head and jaw, regulating the production of hormones, controlling behaviour and activity patterns, and much more. With this in

mind, it is not really surprising that the larger, most active sharks tend to have bigger brains than the slower, bottom-dwellers. Hammerheads have the biggest brains of all, but this does not automatically mean that they are the most intelligent.

The parts of the brain involved in learning and adaptation – the real measures of intelligence – are relatively small. However, experiments in captivity suggest that some sharks can learn surprisingly quickly. Lemon sharks and nurse sharks have been taught to discriminate between coloured discs and different shapes, ring bells in response to offers of food, negotiate mazes, and recover rings from different parts of their tanks. Studies in the wild have shown similar results: shortfin makos quickly learn how to distinguish between different shapes that reward them with either a real fish or an inedible model fish.

There is still much more to discover in this field, and while scientists have identified the basic functions of most parts of a shark's brain, intelligence levels and how they compare with other animals still remain a mystery. But because sharks are sharks rather than people, further investigation into the portions of the brain responsible for analysing the mass of information from the most diverse array of technologically advanced sensors of any predator should perhaps be our first priority.

How do sharks find their way around?

Do they have more than five senses?

What leads sharks to their prey?

Does the sense of smell work under water?

How do sharks hear?

Do sharks see in colour?

What is the 'third eye'?

Do sharks feel pain?

Can ocean currents help sharks to navigate?

How do sharks communicate with one other?

Senses Out of This World

Sensations Beyond Our Imagination

Sharks probably have the most diverse ways of sensing the environment of any predator on the planet. Teeming with a combination of powerful senses as impressive as anything dreamed up for a science-fiction story, they have even been compared to the starship *Enterprise* from *Star Trek*. To find their way around, hunt prey and avoid predators, sharks have all the usual senses of hearing, sight, smell, taste and touch, but also some that are unavailable and unfamiliar to humans. They must experience sensations we simply cannot imagine in ways we cannot really comprehend.

There is strong evidence that no single sense works in isolation: it is a combination of all the different senses working together that makes sharks such efficient and deadly predators. When lemon sharks, for instance, are captured and released several kilometres away, they are able to find their way back to the capture site even if their eyes are covered, their nostrils blocked, or their electro-receptors disrupted with magnets.

The importance of each sense varies from species to species and largely depends on where they live. Sharks living in the dark depths, for instance, have tiny eyes and relatively poor vision, while species living near the surface probably rely on eyesight much more.

In many species, each sense comes into play at a particular distance from the potential food source. Initially sharks use sound, which travels much farther and five times faster in water than it does in air. If they hear something interesting, perhaps several kilometres away, they will investigate. As they get closer, they are likely to pick up a scent trail, which might be blood or another body fluid, perhaps at a distance of several hundred metres. The so-called lateral-line system, which is used to detect vibrations in the water, kicks in as the sharks approach to within 100 m (328 feet) or so. Then, if the water visibility is reasonable, they can make visual contact at a distance of tens of metres. They might bump the target to obtain some tactile information and, if it seems to be edible, attack. They roll back their eyes or cover

them with special membranes, to protect them from flailing teeth and claws, and switch to yet another sense that detects weak electrical signals from the muscles of their prey and guides their jaws directly to the target. Finally, they take an exploratory bite and, if the prey tastes satisfactory, keep feeding.

Hearing

Hearing is one of the longest-range senses used by sharks. Their hearing is acute and enables them to detect sounds from hundreds of metres or even several kilometres away.

Sharks can hear sounds with a frequency range of about 10–1000 hertz, which in human terms would be the equivalent of deep booms of thunder to the higher notes of our own voices (we can hear from 25–16,000 hertz, so there is considerable overlap). But they are most attracted to the rapid and irregular, low-frequency sounds produced by struggling or injured fish (and, indeed, by healthy people when they are playing in the water). These work like a dinner-bell and can attract sharks from a wide area within minutes. They make such an impact on sharks that fishermen in the South Pacific commonly shake coconut rattles under water to produce intermittent bursts of low-frequency sound that attracts them to their boats.

Sharks do not have external ear flaps, which would create turbulence and noise while swimming, but do have inner ears that open to the outside world through tiny holes behind the eyes, one on each side of the top of the head. These holes are called endolymphatic pores and are the only external sign that sharks

Page 44: A blacktip shark cruises along the top of a coral reef in the Bahamas.
Left: This deep-water dwarf shark lives in the dark depths of the Atlantic, where visibility is very poor.
Opposite: Experiments with lemon sharks suggest that no single sense works in isolation.

have ears at all. They lead along narrow tubes, or ducts, to the fluid-filled inner ear, where patches of hair cells are stimulated by vibrations. Sound waves also pass straight through the shark's head which is, in effect, acoustically transparent.

The lower part of the shark's inner ear is for hearing, but the upper part is concerned with balance. There are three semicircular canals – tubes that open into the inner ear – which are at right angles to each other. These are designed to maintain the shark's orientation and balance by registering movement in different planes and sending nerve impulses to the brain.

Smell

The sense of smell is the ability to detect dissolved molecules, whether they are in the air or in water. For a shark, smell is effectively a form of long-distance tasting, the main difference being that the water is 'tasted' by special receptor cells in the nostrils rather than by taste buds inside the mouth.

If we tried to smell under water, we would drown. But a shark's nostrils, unlike our own, are not connected to the respiratory system. They are adapted exclusively for smelling and lead merely into closed sacs near the front of the shark's snout. Each sac is covered by a flap of skin that channels water, along with any dissolved molecules or suspended particles, into a chamber packed with microscopic odour-detecting cells. As all the relevant information is passed to the brain for analysis and recognition, the water flows out again in a continuous stream.

There is evidence to suggest that sharks are quite selective in their smelling abilities. Smells that are not particularly important to them sometimes cannot be detected at all, but they are super-sensitive to significant smells that are relevant to activities such as feeding or breeding.

Sharks have such large olfactory centres in their brains (for analysing smell information) that they can account for as much as two-thirds of the brain's total weight. Not surprisingly, they have some impressive smelling abilities, and their sense of smell is so important to them that they have been dubbed 'swimming noses'. It has even been claimed that certain species, such as grey reef sharks, can detect one part fish extract or blood in 10 billion parts water. Even if their smelling ability is 1000 times less than this particular calculation, it is still the equivalent of detecting a few drops of blood in an Olympic-sized swimming pool (although, of course, this is different from an open-water setting and is dependent on other conditions being just right – but it gives an idea of their extraordinary abilities).

In moving water they are able to detect blood and other body fluids from at least hundreds of metres away, and possibly even farther. Stories of them swimming unerringly towards their victims from dozens of kilometres away are probably exaggerated, but a reasonably large animal, such as a seal, might attract sharks from a radius of a kilometre or two. As well as being able to smell under water, some sharks are also believed to smell the air in their constant search for a meal.

Allied to their acute sense of smell is an ability to detect the direction from which a particular smell is originating. We can tell where sounds are coming from by moving our heads from side to side and judging which ear receives the sounds first. Sharks use their nostrils in a similar way. A smell coming from the left of a shark reaches its left nostril a fraction of a second before it gets to the right one, and this is enough to guide the shark in the appropriate direction. The greater the distance between the nostrils, the better they are for direction-finding, and this may be why hammerhead sharks have such strange elongated heads. When following a scent trail in the water, the shark swings its head from side to side and will often swim over the trail in a zigzag path so that it samples the water for areas of greatest concentration. This allows it to climb the odour gradient and keep on the right track.

Lateral-line system

One of the most extraordinary mechanisms in a shark's arsenal of senses, the lateral-line system enables it to 'hear', or at least detect, vibrations in the water with its whole body.

The lateral lines are special organs lying just beneath the skin, which run all the way from the head to the tail on each side of the body. Connected to the outside by numerous tiny holes in the shark's skin, they consist of fluid-filled canals with tiny sensory 'hair cells' that are triggered by the slightest changes in water pressure. These send millions of nerve signals to the brain every second and enable the shark almost to feel the presence of an object in the water – in a way that has been described as touching at a distance. We have nothing directly equivalent, but perhaps the nearest sensation is feeling the wind on our skin. Try blowing on the back of your hand while moving a finger up and down in the air flow: this is a crude imitation, but gives an idea of how the lateral-line system might work.

The system probably plays an important role for a hunting shark within a radius of about 100 m (328 feet), and makes it acutely aware of every ripple, eddy and vibration in the surrounding water. It is so effective that recent research by Thomas Breithampt at the University of Konstanz in Germany suggests it could even be used to track the slightly disturbed water in the wake of fishes as they swim nearby.

Vision

Light does not travel well through sea water, and visibility can be very poor even close to the surface. Down in the depths it is usually too dark to rely on eyesight to any great extent. Nevertheless, sharks can see fairly well, even in surprisingly dim light, have an excellent field of vision, and many species can even see in colour.

Sharks' eyes are typical of those in most vertebrates. The jelly-filled eyeball is protected within a socket, or orbit, in the skull. Light passes through a transparent window called the cornea at the front of the eyeball. Behind the cornea is the iris, which controls the amount of light entering the eye by opening and closing a ring of muscle forming a hole called the pupil. The light then passes through a hard, ball-shaped lens, through the clear jelly within the eyeball, and shines on to the retina at the back. The retina is a light-sensitive layer containing nerve fibres and millions of microscopic cells called rods and cones. The rods are essential for seeing in dim light, and the cones are necessary for seeing good detail and colour in bright light. Many sharks have eyes that lack cones, and probably see greyish blurred shadows rather than colourful details, but a few species living in clear surface waters do have cones and can probably see in colour; whether they perceive it in the same way we do is not known.

Broadly speaking, sharks' eyes are adapted to cope well in low light and, on average, are roughly ten times more sensitive to light than our own eyes. As they feed mainly during the periods of dusk, night and dawn, this is an especially useful adaptation for them. In fact, their night vision is so good that some experts believe they are able to hunt by starlight. Like mammals, sharks can dilate their pupils, but they also have a mirror-like layer in each eye to boost the available light still further by reflecting it

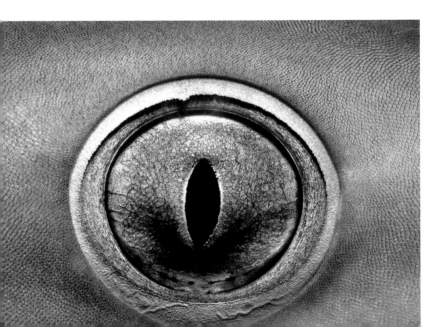

Left: Most sharks have good eyesight, and many species can even see in colour.

back on to the light-sensitive cells in the eye. This *tapetum lucidum* is located behind the retina and effectively doubles the amount of light reaching the photo-receptors in the eye. It is the *tapetum* that makes a shark's eyes shine when they are caught in torchlight on a night dive, rather like cats' eyes caught in car headlights. When the light gets too bright, many sharks are able to protect their eyes by covering the *tapetum* with a curtain of mobile, melanin-filled cells known as melanoblasts. This enables them to rise rapidly from the dimly lit depths into the bright light of surface waters without being blinded. Species living near the surface also have special pigments in their lenses which are believed to help screen out harmful ultraviolet radiation. Deep-water species do not need such protection, and have exceptionally large eyes to help them see in the near-total darkness of the ocean depths, where the only light is often from bioluminescent fish and other marine creatures that make their own light.

Sharks' eyes vary considerably in size, shape and position from species to species. Those living in the ocean depths, for instance, not only have larger eyes than the ones living near the surface, but they can also see in almost all directions. This is because their eyes are set wide apart on the sides of the head, and they swing their heads from side to side while swimming. Some species also have binocular vision immediately in front, enabling them to judge distances fairly accurately, but others have little overlap in the views from the two eyes and therefore do not have this facility. Open-ocean species are believed to be relatively far-sighted, while reef-dwellers are probably a little short-sighted, although recent research suggests that lemon sharks, at least, can focus on both near and distant objects.

Most sharks have upper and lower eyelids, but they do not usually meet in the middle. To protect the eye requiem sharks and some other species have a unique structure called a nictitating membrane, which is a thick, fleshy third eyelid at the bottom of the eye. This can cover the eye completely and protects it when the shark is feeding or in any other potentially hazardous situation. Mackerel sharks, such as great whites, which do not have nictitating membranes, protect their eyes by rolling them up into their sockets just before an attack.

Some sharks have a 'third eye' as well. Known as the pineal window, this is marked by a thin, often pale area on the top of the skull. There is a tiny ball of light-sensitive tissue underneath, which is linked directly to the pineal gland in the brain. It cannot form an image, but is sensitive to light and may help the sharks to regulate their biological clocks and activity cycles. Bottom-dwelling sharks, which use camouflage to blend in with their surroundings, may use information from the third eye to change

Left: These blue sharks are probably using a combination of senses – in ways we can barely imagine – to hunt northern anchovies off the coast of California.

their skin colour. Among deep-sea sharks the third eye may also be used to detect light from the surface to help them as they follow the diurnal vertical migrations of mid-water prey.

Many vertebrates, including humans, have a third eye. Our pineal body is hidden within the brain tissue and is associated with the regulation of our biological clock; it produces serotonin, which converts to the hormone melatonin, the substance partly responsible for jet lag.

Electroreception

Perhaps the most intriguing and mysterious of sharks' senses is the ability to detect the minute amounts of electricity generated by the muscles in all living things. This is a profoundly important sense to sharks, but one that we cannot easily identify with since we have no comparable system.

Sharks have special electrical receptors, called the ampullae of Lorenzini, which are small, jelly-filled pores on the snout and lower jaw. Large enough to be seen with the naked eye, they form a curious pattern of dark holes and look rather like a sparse five-o'clock shadow. Active hunting sharks have 1500 or more ampullae, while sluggish bottom-dwellers tend to have only a few hundred. They were named after the clay jars used by ancient Romans to store grain, oil and wine because the jelly-filled pores resemble their shape. There is some dispute about the person who first discovered the ampullae – whether it was the Italian microscopist Marcello Malpighi in 1663, or the Danish geologist and anatomist Neils Stensen in 1666 – but they were first described in detail by the Italian physiologist Stefano Lorenzini in 1678. It was not until the 1960s, almost 300 years later, that their function was properly understood.

The ampullae of Lorenzini are so effective at detecting weak electrical fields – some estimates suggest as low as five billionths of a volt per centimetre – that a shark can find a prey animal even

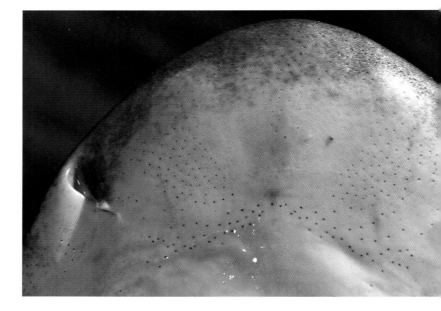

Right: The small, jelly-filled pores visible on the snout and lower jaw of this oceanic whitetip shark are special receptors designed to detect the minute amounts of electricity generated by living muscle.

if it is completely buried in the sand or mud on the seabed. If the animal is not moving, it is still breathing and its heart is pumping, and this results in sufficient muscle activity for the shark to detect the resulting electrical pulses. Even with a conservative estimate of sharks responding to fields of voltage gradients as low as a hundred-millionth of a volt per centimetre, this is the equivalent of a 1.5-volt AA-type battery creating a field between two electrodes set in the sea 1600 km (1000 miles) apart. For comparison, the breathing movements and heartbeat of a resting flatfish, such as a plaice, give off voltages 100,000 stronger. Being in sea water helps enormously: air is a very poor electrical conductor, but water (especially salt water) is good.

The operating range of the electroreceptors is about 30 cm (12 inches), and they are particularly important in the final split second of an attack. Sharks protect their eyes (because they are vulnerable to damage from struggling prey) and are effectively swimming blind just before they hit, so this is when the electrosensory system takes over and guides them the last few centimetres to their target. Hammerheads have their electrical receptors spread across the width of their curiously flattened heads. They are believed to use their heads like metal detectors (except they are detecting electrical fields) by sweeping them back and forth over the sand in search of stingrays and flatfish buried beneath it.

Electroreception might explain why sharks frequently attack divers in safety cages. Rather than trying to get at the divers themselves, they are probably responding to the weak electrical field generated by the metal of the cage. They sometimes mouth boat propellers for the same reason, perhaps mistaking the

electrical field generated by the metal in sea water for muscle activity. This might also explain why sharks often repeatedly attack their original victim, even when there are other people in the water nearby. Wherever the skin is broken there is a much stronger electrical 'aura' (and, of course, more olfactory clues), which is precisely where this remarkable sense guides them.

Touch

The sense of touch is responsible for telling the brain what is in contact with the body and alerting it to specific sensations. We rely on our sense of touch to distinguish between small variations in heat and cold, light and heavy pressure, rough and smooth, dry and wet, hard and soft, and so on. Sharks probably do not have such a sensitive system, perhaps because they rarely make physical contact with objects in the water and do not really need it. But a network of nerve endings beneath the skin can detect a certain amount of basic contact and can probably identify significant changes in temperature and the presence of noxious or corrosive chemicals in the water. It can also detect physical damage.

It is unclear whether sharks feel pain. The fact that they have a reasonable sense of touch suggests that they might feel pain to some degree, but during feeding frenzies, individuals that are seriously injured continue feeding as if nothing has happened. They seem to be unaware that they have been hurt. Some laboratory studies support this theory: several species appear to lack the neuronal machinery considered essential for the perception of pain. Yet for most animals (ourselves included), pain is crucial to survival; it warns us that we are being harmed and gives us the sense to take evasive action. One possibility is that sharks have learned to avoid serious injury by swimming away if a situation is too threatening, so pain therefore serves no useful purpose. This is an interesting field of study and one that is still in its infancy.

Taste

A reasonably good sense of taste helps a shark to decide whether something is edible or not. Taste is probably the least developed sense in sharks, but is important in helping them to select the most appropriate and beneficial prey, and to avoid toxic prey. Once they have located a potential victim, they take a bite to determine its palatability; if it tastes all right, they swallow, and if not, they spit it out immediately.

This probably explains why great white sharks rarely eat people. They prefer animals that are well insulated with a thick layer of high-energy fat, and even the most obese of us could not live up to their high standards. It is far better for them to wait for a seriously blubbery seal than to waste their energy digesting a scrawny human. They take a bite, just to make sure, then spit us out in disgust. Unless the bite severs a major artery, and the victim loses too much blood, there is a reasonable chance of surviving such an attack.

Sharks have microscopic taste buds on bumps scattered around the lining of the mouth and inside the throat. Like us, they can probably distinguish only a few basic flavours – sweet, sour,

salt and bitter. The taste buds are best stimulated by direct contact with the potential food item: some sharks mouth or half-bite to get a taste of their victim, while others take a lump out of it.

As well as taste buds inside the mouth and throat, some species have fleshy, whisker-like structures called 'barbels', which may also be taste organs. They are located near the nostrils and mouth, and feel around for shrimps and other marine invertebrates buried under the sand.

Sharks do have tongues (called basihyals), which are made of relatively inflexible cartilage and lie on the floor of the mouth. In most species the tongue appears to serve no particular purpose, although cookie-cutter sharks use their large, flattened basihyals to create a vacuum to assist their sucker-like mouths when clinging on to their prey.

Navigation

How do sharks migrate across hundreds or even thousands of kilometres of open ocean? How do they know where they are going? For that matter, how do they know when they have arrived? To us, the open ocean appears to be featureless, with few clues to use for navigation. But the clues are there (if only we knew where to look), and, of course, sharks are perfectly tuned in to this underwater world.

The first clues are in the water itself. Ocean currents provide relatively permanent 'landmarks'. Their speed, strength, density, direction of movement, temperature, and physical and chemical make-up can all be used as navigation aids. Sounds in the sea provide more important clues, and recent research suggests that sharks may use the background noise of waves, currents, animals and other sources to build up a sound picture of their surroundings.

But perhaps the most interesting possibility is that sharks use the Earth's magnetic field to navigate. Many animals, from

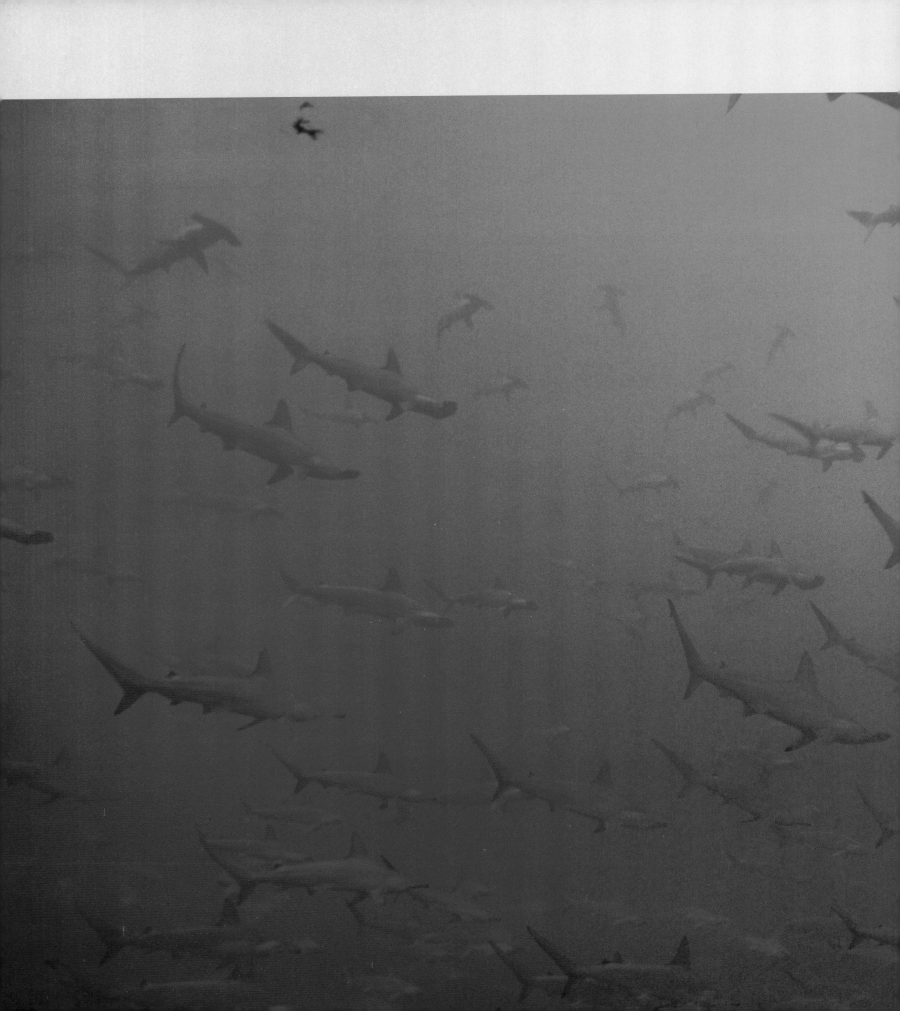

bees to whales, are able to use this field like the contours on a map. Research has revealed tiny crystals of a magnetic material (a form of iron oxide known as magnetite) in the soft tissues covering their brain. One theory is that these crystals continually orientate themselves in line with natural magnetic force fields, rather like tiny compass needles. By sensing changes in the way the crystals are facing, the animals can work out the direction in which they are travelling.

Magnetite has not been found in sharks, but because of the close relationship between magnetism and electricity, they may be able to use their electroreceptors to navigate across vast areas of open ocean. An ocean current creates an electrical field as it flows through the Earth's magnetic field, as does a shark's body, and it is believed that sharks can read the relative fluctuations in these two fields like a map. It seems as if they have their own internal electromagnetic compass, and in some

Above: The painful-looking circular scar on the side of
this dolphin was made by a cookie-cutter shark.
Pages 54–5: A large school of scalloped hammerheads at
Cocos Island, off the Pacific coast of Costa Rica.

species at least this could be their main aid to navigation over long distances.

An ambitious experiment to test this theory was conducted during the 1980s in Bimini in the Bahamas. A ring of electro-magnets was set up in shallow water known to be a popular breeding ground for lemon sharks. The aim was to create the Earth's magnetic field artificially, and sure enough the sharks responded by altering their course accordingly. Every time the artificial field was rotated by 90 degrees, the sharks changed direction by 90 degrees. It was compelling evidence that sharks might rely on the Earth's magnetic field to migrate across vast expanses of open ocean.

Communication

Sharks do not have vocal cords and, with a few exceptions, have no way of vocalizing under water. However, there are reports of whale sharks emitting low, croaking grunts, tasselled wobbegongs coughing as they adjust their grip on prey, and swell sharks barking under water. But the purpose of these sounds, if they really are made, is unknown, and they seem to be the exception rather than the rule. Most sharks have no obvious means of making sounds for communication.

Some experts believe that certain deep-living sharks might use light to communicate. Tiny green lantern sharks, which grow to a length of about 30 cm (12 inches) tend to roam the ocean depths in packs, like underwater wolves. They feed on fishes and squid that are sometimes larger than themselves, suggesting that they co-operate when they are hunting. Scientists believe that the light-producing organs on the sides of their bodies help a hunting pack to communicate in the darkness.

Another way of communicating is by scent. It is possible that sharks release pheromones – chemical compounds that influence the behaviour of other sharks – into the water to signal

their intentions. This could be an effective way of attracting a mate or indicating a readiness to mate, or could be used as a threat or warning.

But compared with many bony fishes, the equipment sharks have for communicating with one another is severely limited. They cannot vocalize; they cannot change colour quickly; their fins are virtually immobile, so they are unable to raise or lower them to change their profile; they cannot erect gill covers or lower their throat to transform the shape of their head; and most of them cannot even twist or turn their bodies. One expert even described them as like mute people running around in straitjackets.

They do, however, communicate with one another using a body language of movements and postures. They have expressionless faces and fairly rigid bodies, so whatever body language they use is likely to be subtle and difficult for us to interpret. But there are some exceptions. Experienced divers have learnt to recognize certain warning signs of a potential attack, or at least to recognize an angry shark. These signs are more marked in some species than others; a grey reef shark, for instance, indicates displeasure by swimming fast or jerkily, swimming in a tight figure-of-eight or tight circles, contorting the body into a distinctive S-shape, arching the back, pushing the pectoral fins downwards, lifting the snout, swinging the head from side to side, and jaw-gaping. A great white shark may show annoyance by gaping its mouth to show its teeth, and perhaps slapping its tail.

Like many animals with dangerous 'weapons', sharks tend to use ritualized displays in social contests, perhaps to avoid getting injured. Studies on great whites suggest that dominant individuals do occasionally bite their subordinates, but they rarely cause serious damage. (Bite marks are commonly seen on great whites, but they are rarely serious gaping wounds.) It makes more sense to settle disputes with displays of strength and threats rather than physical contact.

How do sharks find a partner?

Why do some sharks migrate?

How do male sharks prove their worth?

Is biting a sign of affection?

What happens after fertilization?

Do different species give birth in different ways?

What are 'mermaid's purses'?

Do shark 'nurseries' really exist?

How long do shark pups take to grow up?

Do adult sharks make good parents?

Shark Reproduction
Propagating the Species

In bony fishes, the female lays thousands or even millions of tiny eggs, and these are fertilized by the male outside her body. This is a process known as spawning. Some species look after their fertilized eggs, but most allow them to drift off into the ocean, leaving them to the mercy of the watery environment. Only a fraction of 1 per cent manage to survive long enough to grow up and produce offspring of their own. A female cod, for instance, produces at least 3 million eggs, and the male simply casts his sperm into the sea nearby in the hope that at least some of the eggs will be fertilized.

By the law of averages, at least some eggs spawned by bony fishes will make it. But sharks use a very different strategy.

Sharks mate rather than spawn (in other words, fertilization is internal), they rely on a smaller number of larger eggs (in most species fewer than 100), and many of them keep the eggs safely inside the female's body. This system produces far fewer offspring, but they have a good start in life and a much higher survival rate. In many ways, the system used by sharks is more like the reproductive strategy of birds and mammals than that of other fishes. It is a system that works well in ideal conditions, but it takes time, so is less able to cope with dramatic change. This is why shark populations recover slowly (or not at all) when they are targeted by fishermen or hunters.

Finding a mate

Relatively little is known about courtship and mating in sharks, and these behaviours are rarely observed in the wild. It has been described for only a dozen or so species, and even then, most of the observations have been on captive animals in aquariums or marine laboratories.

The chances of a shark encountering a willing member of the opposite sex are relatively small on a day-to-day basis, especially since sharks tend to live alone or in single-sex groups. So in many species, the breeding process begins with a seasonal migration. Some sharks migrate hundreds or thousands of kilometres from their feeding grounds to suitable breeding grounds. Blue sharks are believed to migrate the farthest, and specimens caught and tagged off the east coast of the United States have been recovered more than 6000 km (3736 miles) away. Limited evidence suggests that some individuals may travel even further.

Little is known of their migrations, although it is clear that there are substantial variations between the movements of adult males, adult females and juveniles. In one population of blue

sharks in the North Atlantic, for example, most of the long-distance travellers are female. They mate off the northeast coast of the USA, then migrate thousands of kilometres across the ocean, following the Gulf Stream and other currents, to drop their pups off the Atlantic coasts of Spain and Portugal. Then they move south along the African coast, before making another transatlantic crossing to the Caribbean. Remarkably, many of these sharks are immature when they begin the journey. They store the sperm until they reach sexual maturity, and their eggs are fertilized some time during their travels. Meanwhile, most of the males simply patrol the eastern seaboard of the USA.

Tiger sharks also routinely travel long distances. Some populations make limited movements into higher latitudes in summer, then back to the tropics in winter. One particular individual, tagged by scientists, spent the summer off the coast of New York and six months later was found off the coast of Costa Rica, 2900 km (1800 miles) away. Shortfin mako follow lines of equal temperature (usually around 18, 19 or 20°C) and, in the winter, travel along so-called thermal corridors between the western North Atlantic, the Caribbean and the Gulf of Mexico.

Making the grade

Males and females do not appear to form long-term bonds – they come together only to mate. The mating season usually lasts for just a week or two, and occurs once a year for most species (although others have to wait for two or three years).

Limited evidence suggests that the females are quite particular about which males they will accept as mates. They are determined to select fit, strong, healthy partners to increase the

Page 58: A tiny swell shark emerges from its egg case.
Opposite: A male silver salmon releases sperm on to eggs laid by a female in the waters of Washington State, USA.

chances of producing fit, strong, healthy offspring. The males, meanwhile, are determined to prove their worth. They take part in dominance displays, and will even attack their subordinates if the competition for a female becomes too intense. The females assess their potential suitors carefully and, if they are not up to scratch, will show their displeasure with body language, such as arching their backs, or by moving away.

One well-studied species is the nurse shark, and literally hundreds of courtings and matings have been observed off the Atlantic coast of the Florida Keys. Scientists have discovered that if unwanted suitors persist, the females sometimes swim into very shallow water, where they turn on to their side, push one pectoral fin into the sand and thrust the other one into the air, making it impossible for the males to grab their fins as a prelude to mating.

Intriguingly, the scientists have also noticed that the females tend to succumb to the advances of the large, dominant males, and positively shun the smaller ones.

Ready or not

It is unclear how the females signal that they are ready to mate, but they probably release pheromones (natural chemical messages) into the water. Male blacktip reef sharks at Walker's Cay in the Bahamas have been observed following females, just as if they are following a scent trail. As soon as the females release pheromones into the water, they may be pursued not just by one but by several different males. This has been observed at a number of shark hotspots around the world. For example, at Cocos Island,

several hundred kilometres off the Pacific coast of Costa Rica, female whitetip reef sharks are sometimes chased, touched, prodded and pushed by gangs of eager males. In some cases, the males appear to be co-operating with each other, and continue harassing a female until one of them manages to mate with her.

Mating can be a brutal affair. The male bites the female on the back, flanks or fins, perhaps to stimulate her and encourage her to co-operate, or perhaps to keep her from slipping away. Most of the wounds inflicted by these mating bites heal fairly quickly,

Opposite: A male whitetip reef shark grabs a female by her pectoral fin as a prelude to mating.
Above: The nurse shark is one of the few species of shark for which courtings and matings have been observed on many occasions in the wild.

but sometimes they can be quite severe. It is believed that even basking sharks retain tiny teeth (which have no purpose in feeding) specifically for the males to hold on to the females during copulation. In some species the females have particularly thick skin (up to three times thicker than in the male), but even this extra protection does not always save them from serious injury.

Another species observed courting and mating in the wild is the sand tiger shark, which has been studied in the wild for about 20 years, ever since a large population was discovered living around the wreckage of sunken ships and submarines off North Carolina, on the Atlantic coast of the USA. This is where the warm waters of the Gulf Stream come closest to the eastern shore, and where they meet the cold waters of the Labrador Current. Sometimes the sharks are alone, often they are in pairs, and

there can be groups of five or six, each shark stacked on top of the other. The females are present all year round, and are joined by the males for the summer. (Males migrate along the eastern seaboard, moving northwards in the spring and returning south in the autumn.) The males bite the females in front of the first dorsal fin before copulation, leaving substantial bite marks and frequently losing some teeth in the process; there are numerous teeth lying around on the sandy seabed to prove the point.

Mating positions

Male sharks have two external reproductive organs, known as claspers, which develop from medial folds in the pelvic fins and are analagous to the penis in mammals. Rolled up like scrolls, they

Above: The claspers (external reproductive organs) show clearly on the underside of this bronze whaler shark.
Opposite: Mating nurse sharks in shallow water off the Florida Keys.

form tubes or channels for discharging the sperm into the female's body. Complete with a stiffening cartilaginous core, they are easy to see and make it relatively simple to differentiate between the sexes. The term 'clasper' was originally coined by Aristotle, who mistakenly believed that males used them to clasp or grab the females. There are, in fact, two main copulating techniques: a small, flexible shark will hang on tightly to his mate by his mouth, then wrap himself around her to mate; a larger species with less flexibility will position himself parallel to the female.

The actual mating position varies from species to species and place to place; it may also vary between individuals. Whitetip reef sharks in Hawaii have been observed mating side by side, with their heads resting on the seabed and their tails pointing at an angle towards the surface. Around Cocos Island they have been observed mating while hanging upside-down in mid-water. And in other parts of the world, observers have witnessed the same species mating while rolling around among rocks and sea urchins.

The male inserts one of his claspers into the female's vent (the slit that leads into the cloaca, which also contains the urinary and anal openings). Which clasper he uses depends on which side of the female he has managed to grasp. Usually, the right clasper is used, but it is not uncommon to use the left; some species actually use both, either at the same time or one after the other. In many species the clasper is firmly anchored inside the cloaca by spines, hooks or ridges to ensure that it does not slip out. The male then discharges the seminal fluid in a jet of sea water squirted out by special muscles in the abdominal wall. Copulation typically lasts for a minute or two. After mating, the males often drop to the seabed from exhaustion and a lack of oxygen (since their jaws have been clinging on to the females' fins for the whole time), and take a while to recover.

There is growing evidence that some females choose several different mates. Researchers studying lemon sharks in Bimini in the Bahamas have found that females have litters of ten to 12 pups with as many as four different fathers. More research is needed, but it is quite possible that multiple paternity may be common in other large sharks too.

Laying eggs and giving birth

Female sharks do not always fertilize their eggs immediately after mating. Sometimes, like blue sharks (see p. 60), they store the sperm for many months or even years before they are ready, and they might even use the sperm from a single mating over several breeding seasons.

When the eggs have been fertilized, the sharks adopt one of two main strategies. The most 'primitive' strategy is oviparity, which involves laying eggs. The embryos are entirely dependent on the yolk reserves inside the eggs for their nourishment. This is the method used by about 40 per cent of known shark species.

The other, more 'advanced' strategy is viviparity, which involves live birth. During the course of evolution, about 60 per cent of shark species have switched to this strategy, probably because life inside the female's body ensures that the young sharks are safe from predation and other hazards. It also provides a temperature-controlled environment and plenty of oxygen until they are sufficiently well developed to fend for themselves.

There are two main forms of viviparity: yolk-sac viviparity (previously known as 'ovoviviparity'), in which the eggs develop inside the mother's uterus and obtain their nutrients mainly (or exclusively) from the yolk; and true viviparity, in which the mother provides the nutrients herself, usually via a placenta.

Opposite: Swell sharks are among many species that
lay eggs; each egg is packaged in a tough case called
a 'mermaid's purse'.

Oviparity

It tends to be the smaller species that lay eggs outside their
bodies. The fertilized eggs pass out of the female's body via the
cloaca and vent, a complex process that can take several hours.
Port Jackson sharks and swell sharks are among many species
that use this system. They package each egg in a tough case or
pouch that is secreted by a special gland. These egg cases vary
considerably in shape: the Port Jackson shark's opaque egg
cases have a spiral flange on the outside; those of the common
dogfish are translucent and almost rectangular; and the egg
cases of the tropical catshark are shaped rather like cuttlefish,
with beautiful ridges along the sides.

Many egg cases have tendrils, which safely anchor them to
rocks or seaweed on the seabed; some have sticky sides, providing
a Velcro-like attachment; and others are corkscrew-shaped, ready
to be anchored in the sand or wedged into a crevice.

Initially, the egg case is pale and soft, but after a few hours
in sea water, it darkens and hardens into a leathery protective
coat. The embryo can still be clearly seen inside. A female
California horn shark will actually pick up the soft, freshly laid
egg cases in her mouth and deposit them in crevices so that when
they harden they are firmly wedged. Port Jackson sharks are
believed to drive their eggs firmly into place by holding one end
in the mouth and working it into the crevice with an action similar
to using a screwdriver. Time spent securely fastening and hiding
the eggs significantly improves the chances of the developing
embryos escaping attacks by sea snails and other predators, or
being washed away by the sea.

Each developing embryo has its own exclusive egg case with
its own egg yolk, and it is totally dependent on this for survival.

It is attached to the membrane of the yolk sac by an umbilical
cord, through which it obtains all the sustenance it needs. The
case has small respiratory holes, and the embryo actually controls
the amount of oxygen inside by managing the flow of water
through them. When it is fully developed, and the time comes to
emerge, the young shark has to break out of its egg case and
wriggle free. A baby swell shark has two rows of large dermal
denticles down its back, which it uses to tear a hole in the tough
protective shield; these denticles are shed when the shark is out
in the open water. Empty egg cases often wash ashore, especially
after a storm, and these are the so-called 'mermaid's purses'
commonly found by beachcombers.

Yolk-sac viviparity

Yolk-sac viviparity is a mid-way strategy between oviparity and
true viviparity and this is the system used by most species,
including tiger sharks, nurse sharks and shortfin makos. The eggs
develop within the relative safety of the mother's uterus and
hatch inside her body. The female spiny dogfish, for instance,
typically has five developing embryos stacked inside a long, thin
membraneous container (known as a 'candle' because of its
shape). There is one container in each of her two uteri. After
about six months the candle disintegrates, but each embryo
keeps its original egg sac and continues to grow inside the
uterus. In every species adopting yolk-sac viviparity, each pup
has its own yolk sac for nourishment, and it 'hatches' out of a
membraneous covering (rather like cling-film) before being born.

In most cases, it is believed that the embryos receive no
nutrition directly from the mother. They live on food supplies
inside their eggs and develop in exactly the same way as in egg-
laying sharks. But there are exceptions. Some species do not give
birth as soon as the embryos have hatched from their temporary
homes, but keep them inside the uterus and provide extra

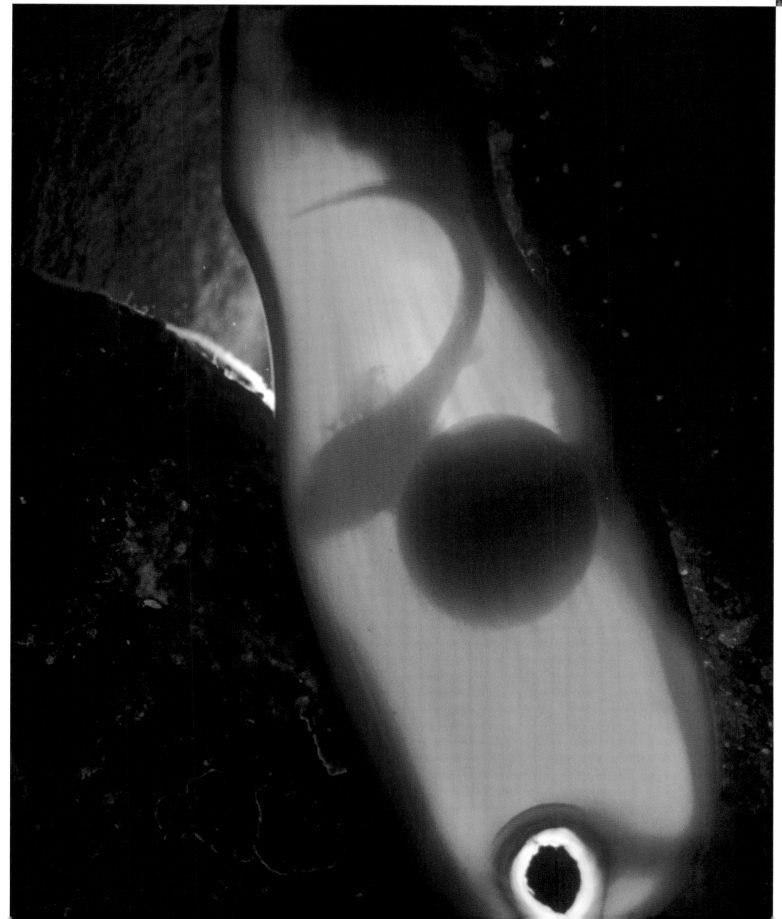

sustenance until they are even bigger, stronger and better prepared to face the outside world. The females of mackerel sharks, such as the great white, and some other species, continue to ovulate unfertilized eggs after the first embryos have hatched in order to provide an additional source of food for them. Tiger shark embryos each feed from their own yolk sac, but they are also provided with a kind of creamy uterine 'milk' that is secreted from the walls of the mother's uterus.

Sometimes the developing pups find their own food. The first-hatched pups of sand tiger sharks quickly use up the food in their yolk sacs and promptly start dining on their smaller siblings, a behaviour known as uterine cannibalism. When they have eaten their siblings, their mother continues to ovulate and the sharks feed on her steady stream of unfertilized eggs until they are ready to face the outside world. Eventually, the two dominant pups are born, one from each of the two uteri.

There have been decades of debate about whether whale sharks use yolk-sac viviparity or lay eggs. The controversy began on 29 June 1953, when an enormous egg case 30 cm (12 inches) long, 14 cm (5½ inches) wide and 9 cm (3½ inches) deep) was found by a fisherman trawling for shrimps in the Gulf of Mexico. The case contained a living whale shark embryo, some 35 cm (14 inches) long. Scientists could not agree whether the egg case had been deposited naturally and the embryo was developing inside, or whether something had gone wrong and its mother had aborted her offspring prematurely. The dispute was not resolved until 1995, when a 10.7-m (35-feet) pregnant whale shark was harpooned by Taiwanese fishermen. Scientists found no fewer than 300 embryos in the uteri, ranging in length from 41 cm (16 inches) to 65 cm (26 inches). Most were in egg cases, each with a yolk sac, but the largest had already hatched and were still inside their mother's body. As well as solving the dispute – it was proof that whale sharks are yolk-sac viviparous – this was also the largest number of embryos found in any shark.

Viviparity

The most advanced reproduction strategy is true viviparity. Bull sharks, blue sharks, hammerheads and other members of the Carcharhinidae family (requiem sharks) have developed a system that is quite remarkable for fishes. Viviparity in these more 'modern' sharks is almost identical to our own live-bearing strategy, although it evolved millions of years earlier. Just as in mammals, the females actually become pregnant. The embryos remain inside the mother and survive for the first few months by using food from the yolk sac. The spent sac then makes a connection with the uterine wall, forming the yolk-sac placenta, which serves exactly the same function as the placenta in mammals, providing nourishment and oxygen directly from the mother's bloodstream to the developing embryos. The embryos of scalloped hammerheads rely on their yolk sac for food initially, but then the sac attaches itself to the mother's uterine wall and begins to extract nutrients directly from the mother's bloodstream. Waste products from the embryo are transferred back the other way to the mother for removal. When the pups are born, they have to thrash about to break the umbilical cord that still connects them to the placenta, and the mother has to expel an afterbirth, consisting of the placenta and embryonic membranes.

Gestation periods vary enormously, with some smaller sharks taking as little as five to six months, and most large ones nine to 12 months. The gestation period in tiger and blacktip sharks may be as long as 16 months, while in basking sharks it could be two years. Another long gestation period is found in the spiny dogfish; after spending six months inside their candles, the embryos emerge to develop for another 14 months or so, still inside their mother's body. The total gestation period is therefore 20–22 months. Gestation periods also vary between individuals within a species. There is no precise gestation time since most sharks are cold-blooded, so the rate at which the embryos develop depends

partly on the temperature of the surrounding water. In swell sharks, for instance, embryo development takes about seven months in relatively warm water and as long as ten months if the water is cold. There is some evidence that certain sharks will seek out warm water just to speed up the growth of their embryos. It is believed that grey reef sharks enter shallow lagoons in the South Pacific, especially during the middle of the day and early afternoon when the sun is at its hottest, for this reason.

One species, the Australian sharpnose shark, is unique in keeping its developing embryos in a state of 'suspended animation'. Studies in Cleveland Bay, Queensland, reveal that the sharks mate during the summer and, initially, the embryos develop quite normally. But they stop developing for about seven months, then start again as if nothing has happened. Eventually, the litter of about ten pups is dropped several months later.

Above: A newborn lemon shark enters the world in a shallow lagoon in the Bahamas.

Many sharks give birth in special nursery areas, often close to shore in shallow lagoons, bays or estuaries, where there is plenty of food for their newborn pups and where they are relatively safe from larger sharks. For a short period during the summer months, for instance, literally hundreds of nurse sharks gather in the shallows off French Cay in the Turks and Caicos Islands to mate and lay their eggs. Another favourite shark breeding ground is a lagoon in Bimini, in the Bahamas, where female lemon sharks go to pup every spring and early summer. The young sharks remain inside the lagoon until they are seven or eight years old, when they are large enough to head out towards the open reef. Some species, however, give birth in the open ocean, far offshore, or on the ice-cold, deep-sea floor. Big sharks, such as shortfin makos, give birth to youngsters that are large and strong enough to hunt and look after themselves in the dangerous open sea almost as soon as they are born.

Birth is usually a rapid process, perhaps to protect the emerging pup from predators waiting to take advantage of its

disorientation and inexperience. Most shark pups are born tail-first, as a precaution against complications during birth (they stand a better chance of survival if the head is still protected inside the mother's body), but sand tigers, scalloped hammerheads and some other species are born head-first. The characteristic 'wings' of the hammerhead shark's head are soft and pliable in newborn pups, an adaptation to make birth easier. Some species with dorsal spines have special protective caps over the spines to make the birth less painful; the caps drop off soon afterwards.

The number of youngsters produced varies considerably between species, from as few as one in each uterus of the bigeye thresher to more than 100 in blue sharks and bluntnose sixgill sharks. Great whites have up to ten pups, oceanic whitetips

between six and nine, nurse sharks have up to 30, and tiger sharks around 40 (but as many as 82) in a single litter.

The size of the newborn pup also varies considerably, from a few centimetres in some lantern sharks to 1.2 m (4 feet) in great whites, and as much as 1.8 m (6 feet) in basking sharks. The pups are small but slightly slimmer versions of their parents – complete with a full set of teeth – and are able to swim and feed almost immediately after birth or hatching. This is important because their first challenge is to escape from their mothers. If they hang around for too long, there is a good chance that their cannibalistic parents will try to eat them (although there is evidence that the females of some species may suppress the urge to feed while they are in the pupping area).

Parental care

There are some impressive examples of parental care in certain bony fishes, even though most of them fertilize their eggs externally and produce hundreds, or even thousands, of eggs at a time. Some of the best examples are the nest-guarding and mouth-breeding behaviours seen in cichlids and sticklebacks.

Sharks invest considerable time and energy into producing strong, resilient offspring and go to a lot of trouble to lay their eggs or give birth somewhere safe. But in most cases they show no interest after the pups have been born. They swim away and leave them to fend for themselves. When a lemon shark pup leaves its mother's body, for instance, the umbilical cord breaks, it swims away to fend for itself, and it has no contact with its mother or any of its siblings ever again.

However, there is limited evidence to suggest that there may be exceptions. Adult scalloped hammerheads in the Red Sea have been observed apparently forming protective shields around their youngsters. And at Ningaloo Reef in Western Australia, a female whale shark was observed from the air, by a shark expert in a light aircraft, surrounded by what appeared to be 14 baby whale sharks. Much more research is needed before we understand fully the extent of parental care in these and other shark species.

Growing up

Sharks are slow-growing animals and take a long time to reach maturity. Generally, the longer a shark lives, the later in life it matures. Some larger species are not ready to breed until they are in their late teens, and male whale sharks are probably not able to do so until they are 20 or 30. There is even a population of spiny dogfish in which the females do not reach sexual maturity until they are at least 35 years old.

Male and female sharks often grow at roughly the same rate, but eventually the females outstrip the males and grow larger.

Both longer and bulkier, a female can weigh one-quarter as much again as a male. Location has an influence too. Tiger sharks, for instance, grow considerably faster (at least for the first four years) in the Gulf of Mexico than in the northwest Atlantic.

It is possible to estimate the age of a shark by counting the growth rings in its spinal column, like counting the rings on a tree. But this is not an easy or precise science because the rings grow throughout their lives, the rate of growth slows after sexual maturity, one year's growth may be marked by several bands rather than one seasonal band, and different species grow at different rates. The most useful information comes from tagging programmes, simply because there is often a long gap of many years or even decades between the original capture of the shark and its subsequent recapture.

What we do know is that lifespans of sharks vary widely, depending on the species and even on where they live. Bull sharks, shortfin makos and grey reef sharks probably live for about 25 years or more, but other species have much shorter or longer lifespans. The whale shark is believed to be one of the longest lived, reaching 100 or even 150 years, and some experts even claim that it is one of the longest-living animals on the planet.

Opposite: A juvenile silvertip shark swims alongside an adult of the same species – perhaps evidence of parental care.
Below: A juvenile blacktip reef shark in a shallow lagoon in the Maldives.

Why are sharks adapted to a 'feast or famine' regime?

What is so special about shark teeth?

How do shark jaws work?

Do hunting techniques vary between species?

What role does camouflage play?

Do sharks believe in teamwork?

Are there any vegetarian sharks?

What are sharks' favourite foods?

Do sharks eat each other?

Who dares to prey on sharks?

Why do sharks turn their stomachs inside out?

The Ultimate Predator
Always on the Lookout for Food

Sharks are often described as the ultimate killing machines. This may be a rather sensational description, but there is no escaping the fact that they are remarkable and highly efficient – some would say near-perfect – predators. A far cry from the mindless monsters they were once believed to be, they are equipped with a sophisticated and awe-inspiring array of sensory mechanisms to track down their quarry, and armed with formidable and powerful weaponry to tackle a wide variety of prey. Quite simply, they are outstandingly good at what they are designed to do.

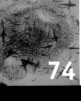

Most sharks feed on small- to medium-sized fish, but as a group they will eat almost anything, including whale carcasses, dolphins, seals, albatrosses, sea turtles, stingrays, squid, crabs, sea urchins and microscopic plankton. They have an equally wide range of hunting techniques to match such a diversity of prey, from chasing fast-swimming animals in the open ocean and waiting in ambush to scavenging and filter-feeding.

Despite their ravenous reputation, most sharks are not particularly big eaters. Unlike humans, who tend to feed in response to pangs of hunger, they seem to be a little hungry all the time. They have a continuous low-level drive to feed, and, although always cruising around on the lookout for food, do not appear to become seriously roused to eat until they actually detect something edible. They seem to be adapted to a 'feast or famine' regime, gorging themselves almost to bursting point when they can, but then going for days, weeks or even months without another meal. On average, a shark must eat between 0.6 and 3 per cent of its body weight each day. Nurse sharks and other sluggish species are at the lower end of the scale, while shortfin makos need much more food to compensate for their high-speed chases. A 64-kg (140-lb) mako must eat at least 1.8 kg (4 lb) of fish each day to survive, and much more if it has

been very active. A shark might eat its own weight in food roughly once a month, whereas a carnivorous bony fish is more likely to take just three or four days to eat the equivalent amount.

Teeth

Sharks are perhaps best known for their impressive teeth. Their shape, size and number vary enormously from one species to another, depending on the diet. Some sharks have as many as 3000 teeth, others only a few dozen. In general terms, surface-feeding sharks tend to have sharp teeth to seize and hold soft-bodied, struggling prey, while at the other extreme, bottom-feeding sharks have flattened teeth for crushing the shells of shellfish and crustaceans. But the teeth can be large or small, broad-based or narrow-based, sharp or blunt, serrated or smooth, and single-cusped or multi-cusped. They are so distinctive that a species can often be identified by a single tooth, or even by its tooth marks in a shark-attack victim.

Tiger sharks have heavily serrated, cockscomb-shaped teeth resembling the teeth in a circular saw, and by moving their mouths in a rolling motion can even bite through mammalian bone and the tough shells of large sea turtles. Frilled sharks have strange broad-based teeth with three sharp cusps separated by two intermediate cusps, probably for feeding on deep-water fishes and squid. Sand tiger sharks have long, pointed, needle-sharp teeth designed for grasping slippery fishes and squid, while whale sharks and basking sharks have tiny, vestigial teeth that appear to serve no dietary purpose (they may be used by the male

Page 72: Silky sharks attacking a bait ball of young jacks in the North Pacific.
Above: The jaw of a nurse shark showing row after row of uniquely shaped replacement teeth.
Opposite: A tiger shark takes a large bite from a marlin carcass in Australia.

as they grow older, their teeth change quite dramatically. Adult great whites have large, serrated, triangular teeth resembling arrowheads in the upper jaw, to saw through the flesh and bones of their mammalian prey, but have slightly longer, more pointed teeth in the lower jaw, for holding the prey steady. We use a similar combination when using a knife and fork.

In many other species, a single shark may have several different kinds of teeth, designed appropriately for catching, cutting or crushing their food. The teeth in the lower jaw of the dusky shark, for instance, are straight and pointed to grab and hold on to its prey, while those in the upper jaw are serrated, asymmetrical and triangular to cut through the prey. The goblin shark has an extraordinary elongated snout, flattened into the shape of a paddle, with long and narrow teeth at the front for grasping fishes and squid, and small, flattened teeth at the back for crushing and grinding shellfish and sea urchins. The grey reef shark has similar narrow, pointed teeth in its lower jaw for holding on to slippery prey, but curved teeth in the upper jaw to pull the prey back into its mouth. In other species, such as some catsharks in the genus *Halaelurus*, tooth shape varies between the sexes.

Sharks' teeth are enlarged versions of the skin scales, or dermal denticles, that cover most of their bodies. They are made of a hard, shock-absorbing substance called dentine, which is covered by an even harder layer of a substance similar to enamel. In the centre is a pulp cavity with blood vessels and nerves. The roots are loosely embedded in a fibrous mass known as the tooth bed – not in the jaws. The tooth bed sits on the jaw cartilage, and the teeth are held in place by fleshy gums.

In a conveyor-belt process, sharks' teeth are continually being shed and replaced with new ones. Behind each functional tooth is a replacement, ready to move into position as soon as the first one is worn, broken off or lost. Behind the replacement is another developing tooth, and so on. Replacement teeth are usually folded down against the gums, beneath a skin-like

to hold on to the female during mating). For its body size, the largetooth cookie-cutter shark has the largest teeth of any known shark – used to cut out an oval-shaped plug of flesh from prey much larger than itself. Intriguingly, perhaps because calcium is scarce in its deep-water home, the cookie-cutter has the curious habit of swallowing its own teeth when they are old or broken.

In some species the tooth shape changes with age, adapting to different hunting habits. Young sharks tend to take small, easy-to-catch prey, but move on to larger, more-difficult-to-catch prey later in life. Juvenile and immature great whites under about 3 m (10 feet) have pointed teeth for grabbing slippery fishes, but

membrane, and move forward and upright only when they are needed. Austrian diving pioneer Hans Hass dubbed them 'revolver teeth' because of the shark's ability to replace them rapidly, like the bullets in a gun. It means that they always have brand-new, razor-sharp teeth ready for action.

In most species, the teeth are replaced one by one, rather than all at once. The process begins as soon as the shark develops inside its egg case or inside its mother, and continues until death. The speed of tooth replacement depends upon the species, the age of the individual, the season and environmental factors, such as water temperature. Nurse sharks lose a row of teeth roughly once every eight days during the summer, when feeding is good, but only once every couple of months in winter, when there is less to eat. In total, lemon sharks are believed to produce – and lose – no fewer than 40,000 teeth in their 50-year lifespan.

Jaws

A shark's teeth would be almost useless without a good set of jaws and powerful jaw muscles to swing them into action. The jaws are attached to the skull only by muscles and elastic ligaments, enabling some species to throw them forward, like an outstretched arm, and open them very wide. Consequently, some sharks are able to bite off lumps of flesh that are far too big to swallow. A great white shark can easily cut a 10-kg (22-lb) chunk of blubber from a whale carcass in a single bite.

The jaws of most sharks are slung apparently awkwardly underneath the head, and for many years it was believed that this forced them to turn on one side or upside-down immediately before attacking their prey. But both the upper and lower jaws are loose and moveable. When a great white shark attacks, it lifts its snout up and back, dropping its lower jaw to open its mouth as wide as possible, then forcing its upper jaw forward (a startling and terrifying sight). The lower jaw hits the target first (an elaborate system of shock-absorbing joints protect the skull and spinal column from the power of impact), and the upper jaw bites down with enough force to shear off a slice of flesh.

Sharks' jaws are powerful, although many of the figures quoted for the force of their bite are nonsense. It is difficult to make a direct comparison, but studies have shown that the biting force of most species does not appear to be much more impressive than it is in humans. Bite strengths have been measured scientifically, using a wonderfully named device called a gnathodynamometer. There are many variations on the basic design of this machine, but, in its simplest form, it consists of a metal or plastic plate of known hardness, which is placed inside a piece of fish or some other suitable bait. When the shark bites on the plate, the tooth indentations can be used to calculate the force of the bite per unit area. It has been found that sharks have a maximum biting force of 60 kg (132 lb), compared with an average of 45-68 kg (100-150 lb) in people – although some Inuit have an exceptionally strong biting force of up to 160 kg (352 lb). The difference, of course, lies in the teeth: a shark's mouthful of razor-sharp teeth can cause considerably more damage than a human's small number of relatively blunt teeth. This is how a tiger shark is able to bite through hard turtle shell.

But not all sharks need a powerful bite. The Port Jackson shark, for instance, eats hard-shelled prey such as shellfish and sea urchins. Its jaws are arranged in such a way that they can move against each other – forwards, backwards and sideways – and this, together with their flattened teeth, forms a powerful grinding mill.

Opposite: Revealing its impressive teeth and jaws, a great white shark breaches off the coast of South Africa.
Right: The longnose sawshark feeds by trailing its barbels along the seabed to locate small fishes.

Hunting techniques

Sharks have an impressive range of hunting techniques, depending on where they live and their favourite prey.

Many reef sharks are benthic foragers, living on or near the seabed and moving over wide areas of reef or open sandy bottoms in search of food. The nurse shark spends most of its time on or near the seabed, and can use its long pectoral fins to 'walk' on the bottom, to 'stand up' and even to reverse out of tight spots. In most parts of the world, it is sluggish during the day, typically lying motionless with its head hidden under a ledge or inside a cave, and sometimes even lying on top of other nurse sharks. But it becomes more active at night, feeding with the help of whisker-like barbels on its snout, which detect or 'taste' for the presence of marine invertebrates buried in the sand. If it finds a likely-looking animal hiding out of reach, it cups its mouth over the hole or crevice and then, by expanding its throat, creates a vacuum that sucks the hapless creature out.

The whitetip reef shark is also fairly sluggish and seems to spend most of the day lounging around, resting on the seabed or in crevices in coral reefs. Several individuals may lie together in a row, or share a bolthole. But when it is time to feed, they go their

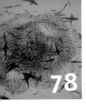

separate ways and become relentless, competitive predators. They hunt mostly at night, when many of the smaller reef inhabitants are asleep in holes in the reef. They are not good at catching prey animals in open water, so tend to specialize in extracting them from their resting places. They may break apart coral heads to get at reef fishes and invertebrates, and their well-protected bodies are so flexible that they can wriggle into tiny crevices and holes, only to emerge from another crevice or hole on the other side of the reef. It is not unusual to see several whitetip reef sharks piling into a single hole and scrabbling furiously to extricate the unfortunate victim hiding inside.

Other benthic species, such as Pacific angelsharks, are ambush predators. The Pacific angelshark is a flattened shark, often mistaken for a ray, with a camouflaged body that helps it to blend in perfectly with its sandy home. It lies on the sea floor, buried in the sand with only its head and eyes exposed, waiting in ambush. As soon as an unsuspecting fish or squid passes nearby, it suddenly bursts out of its hiding place, rears up and sucks the hapless victim straight into its mouth.

Many skilled exponents of the surprise attack use trickery to lure unsuspecting reef fishes much closer. Wobbegongs in the family Orectolobidae blend in with their backgrounds even better than the angelsharks. For example, the tasselled wobbegong is so perfectly camouflaged with the help of fleshy tassels and a cryptic pattern of spots, stripes and blotches on its back that it looks just like seaweed. When it lies motionless in ambush, it is almost impossible to see. Its camouflage is so good that its prey does not always just pass by – sometimes it is lured even closer, thinking that the wobbegong is a safe shelter. All the shark has to do is open its mouth and the victim is sucked into the resulting vacuum;

Opposite: Tiger sharks are the ultimate scavengers and opportunists – this one is tackling a Laysan albatross at Midway Atoll, Hawaii.

there are plenty of sharp, needle-like teeth to stop its escape.

Great hammerhead sharks have a particular penchant for stingrays and it is not uncommon to see a great hammerhead covered in their barbs: one individual was reputed to have no fewer than 96 of them embedded in its head, mouth and throat. The hammerhead uses its broad, flattened head to pin a stingray against the seabed, and then twists around and cleanly bites off a large chunk of the animal's pectoral fin or 'wing'. Once the stingray has been immobilized, the shark takes more leisurely bites. Thresher sharks are instantly recognizable by their enormous, scythe-like tails – it is the upper lobe that is exceptionally long, and may equal the whole length of the body – and these are used as weapons, like whips, to herd or stun prey animals, such as fishes or squid. The sharks swim around a shoal in ever-decreasing circles, lashing out to herd their prey together. Then they rush in, swatting and swiping, before turning back to swallow their stunned or dead victims. Their jaws are relatively small, but their sharp teeth are very efficient at capturing such slippery prey.

Great whites seem to be strongly visual predators and are among the few fishes known to 'spyhop' – lift their heads out of the water, apparently to look around for prey. They will hunt deep-diving elephant seals, but many attacks on seals take place at the surface, without warning, from below and behind. Sometimes they leap right out of the water in pursuit.

Other sharks are pursuit predators that use speed and manoeuvrability to chase down their fleeing prey. The ultimate example is the fastest shark known, the shortfin mako, which is capable of overtaking swordfish and other champion ocean swimmers. Determining how fast a shark (or any other fish) can swim is notoriously difficult, and all sorts of exaggerated claims have been made, but it can probably reach speeds of 35–56 km/h (22–35 mph). Like the great white and several other mackerel sharks, the shortfin mako has a sophisticated modification of its

circulatory system, which effectively makes it warm-blooded. (The extremities remain cool, but the core temperature is warmed.) By retaining body heat, the muscles are bathed in warm blood (about 5–7°C/40–44°F above the temperature of the surrounding water). This is an adaptation for fast, efficient swimming and gives the mako an advantage over its cold-blooded prey.

Filter-feeders thrive by straining microscopic plants and animals from huge volumes of water. There are three species of plankton-feeding sharks, and, although they are not closely related, they have evolved similar methods of feeding. Despite their size, basking sharks feed on tiny plankton floating near the surface of the water in cold temperate regions of the world. They do not use their teeth at all for feeding. They cruise slowly at a speed of about 3 km/h (2 mph), with their mouths wide open, and capture the tiny creatures in special sieves. These are formed by thousands of filters called gill rakers, which remove particulate

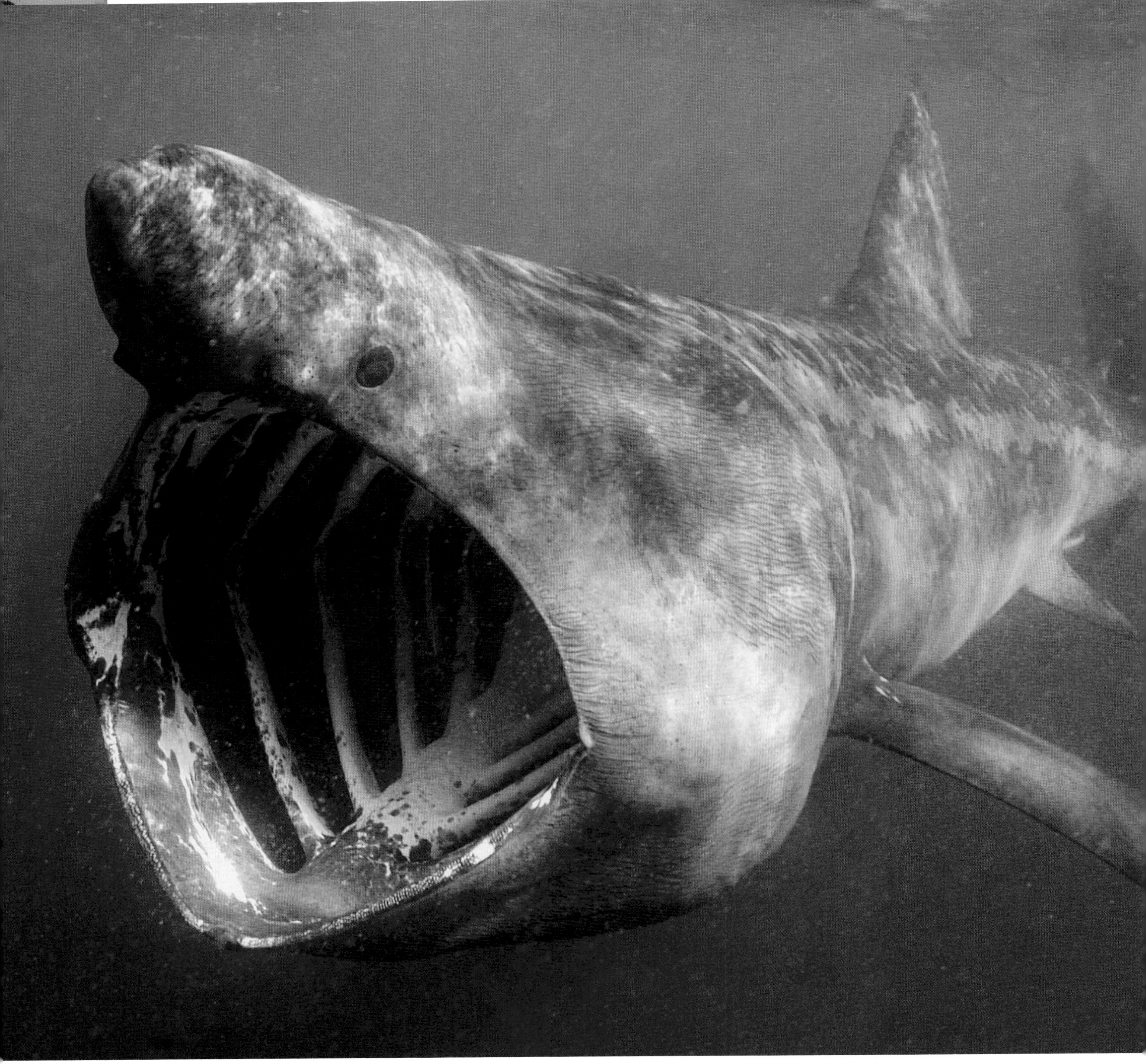

Opposite: The basking shark is essentially an industrial-sized mouth with fins, and feeds by filtering tiny planktonic animals from the sea.

matter from the water as it passes through the gill slits. It is an efficient system – so efficient, in fact, that experts estimate a single basking shark can filter enough sea water to fill a 50-m (164-feet) Olympic swimming-pool every hour.

Whale sharks are also highly efficient filter-feeders, roaming the warm temperate and tropical waters of the world following seasonal concentrations of food. They swim slowly near the surface, scooping up shoals of zooplankton in their open mouths, or remain stationary and vacuum up larger, more dynamic prey, such as sardines and anchovies. Although they are the largest fish in the sea, they have surprisingly small throats and cannot swallow anything larger than a small tuna. The third filter-feeder is the megamouth shark, which patrols much deeper waters in the open ocean. It is believed to spend the day swimming slowly through the gloom, filtering bioluminescent shrimps, pancake jellies, copepods and other small invertebrates from the water, and then moves up to within about 15 m (50 feet) of the surface at night. Its cavernous mouth has a reflective silvery lining, which may encourage unwary prey animals to swim inside.

Competitors or co-operators?

Whether sharks ever co-operate in their never-ending quest for food, or just happen to come together at a good source of food and are therefore competing with one another instead, is still a matter of debate. Wherever there is a large quantity of food, such as a whale carcass or a densely packed shoal of fish, there are likely to be large numbers of sharks present. But they are not necessarily working as a team: they feed together merely because the food is there. Large groups of whale sharks or basking sharks,

for instance, are commonly encountered in areas rich in plankton, but they are probably working independently of one another.

Co-operative feeding has been reported in sandbar sharks, porbeagles and several other species, and recent research suggests that some of them actively hunt in packs. The spiny dogfish, which itself forms extremely large schools, belongs to a group of sharks named for their habit of hunting together, like wild dogs. However, their behaviour seems to be based on a set of instinctive responses rather than on past experience, advance planning and decision-making. Silky sharks and dusky sharks are more interesting because they seem to work together in a way that goes beyond mere instinct. They surround a shoal of fishes and corral them into a tight ball, then take it in turns to dart into the middle to grab a mouthful. They co-operate and share the food for several minutes, until there are no longer enough fishes in the shoal to make it worth the effort.

There is even evidence of co-operation between sharks and other fishes. Whitetip reef sharks and jack fish may work together in hunting smaller schooling fishes: the jacks attack first, then, when their victims attempt to hide in the reef, the sharks probe them out or drive them into the jaws of their waiting comrades.

There are rules in shark society, and in many species there appears to be a distinct hierarchy at good feeding sites. Generally speaking, smaller individuals wait for their larger relatives to eat their fill. There may be some squabbling, threatening and biting if two sharks try to eat the same piece of food or the competition gets too intense, but there is usually some degree of order. Sharks rarely lose control, despite what we are led to believe by the cinema and popular press. However, they have been provoked into biting at anything and everything around them – including one another – during artificial feedings or when large numbers of people have been in the water after a shipwreck. As more sharks arrive, the tension mounts, excitement levels escalate and they panic in case other sharks steal their food. They are reacting abnormally – over-reacting – to super-normal stimuli that they have probably never come across before. But these 'feeding frenzies' are rarely encountered under natural conditions.

Most sharks go out of their way to avoid unnecessary competition. In a coral reef system, for instance, different species inhabit different parts of the reef and occupy different ecological niches. Grey reef sharks live in the deeper waters on the seaward side of the reef; they live alone or in groups of several dozen or more, and at dusk and dawn move up from the depths to cruise the edge of the reef, where they pin schools of fishes against the wall. Whitetip reef sharks feed among the nooks and crannies of the reef itself, while blacktip reef sharks hunt in groups over the relatively shallow coral reef flats.

Favourite foods

Sharks are all carnivorous. There are no truly herbivorous or plant-eating members of the group (although the filter-feeders consume a rich soup of plankton, which includes microscopic plants as well as animals).

Many of them prefer small- to medium-sized fishes, and invertebrates such as squid and octopuses. Galápagos sharks, for instance, will eat little else. Bottom-dwellers, such as the California hornshark, include crustaceans, sea urchins and molluscs in their diet, and deep-water sharks, such as the Greenland shark, gouge large chunks of flesh from dead whales and seals as they sink towards the seabed. Most are quite cosmopolitan in their diets and will take whatever is available or in season at the time. As well as tackling venomous stingrays, great hammerheads also seem to be undeterred by the poisons found in pufferfish and trunkfish, and will take much larger prey. Other sharks frequently appear on the menu and one great hammerhead in the Bahamas, measuring some 4.5 m (15 feet) long, had a 2.7 m (9 feet) lemon shark in its stomach.

Great white sharks are particularly fond of seals and use stealth and surprise to catch them – accelerating from a cruising speed of about 3 km/h (2 mph) to nearly 25 km/h (16 mph). But they will take a wide variety of other prey in different parts of the world, including dolphins and porpoises, grey whale calves, many different bony and cartilaginous fishes, sea turtles, seabirds, squid and whale carcasses.

The ultimate scavenger and opportunist is the tiger shark, a large, powerful shark often described as the great white of the tropics. Prepared to eat anything at any time, it probably has the widest-ranging diet of all sharks. It has a large stomach capacity and a wide mouth capable of devouring enormous chunks of food. There is very little that tiger sharks will not eat – from highly venomous sea snakes and armour-plated sea turtles to fishes, squid and crustaceans. Ever alert to feeding opportunities, large numbers of them even move into the lagoon at Midway Atoll in

Hawaii for a few weeks every summer to feed on newly fledged albatrosses. They will swallow anything that has fallen or been dropped into the sea, and have been credited with eating all manner of bizarre foods, including the head of a crocodile, old boots, life jackets, coils of wire, boat cushions and beer cans. They also frequent inshore waters close to slaughterhouses, where they feed on the carcasses of sheep, pigs, cows and horses after they have been dumped in the sea. Given the opportunity, many sharks will scavenge. Blue sharks and dusky sharks, for instance, will follow ships at sea, somehow anticipating a free meal when the crew jettison their garbage overboard.

The only known parasitic sharks are the cookie-cutter and its close relative the largetooth cookie-cutter. They are small sharks, reaching a maximum length of 50 cm (20 inches) and 1 m (40 inches) respectively, but have formidable, razor-sharp teeth. They spend the day in deep water, feeding on deep-sea shrimps

and lanternfish. (They are thought to be the most luminescent of all sharks – their light-producing organs probably glow in the dark depths to lure fast-swimming prey close by.) But at night they turn into opportunistic parasites and rise to the surface in search of more substantial prey. They will tackle anything from tuna and swordfish to whales and dolphins, and have even been known to attack the rubberized dome of a nuclear submarine. The tiny sharks dart in and clamp on to the skin of their victims with their sucker-like mouths and huge razor-sharp teeth. Then they twist around and cut out a plug of flesh, just like an ice-cream scoop, or a cookie-cutter being used to cut out a disc of pastry. The temporary host is not killed by the shark, but the attack is

Overleaf: Sharks gather at Cape Cuvier in Australia to feed on the seasonal shoals of anchovies.
Below: A great white shark bursts out of the water as it captures a Cape fur seal pup off the coast of South Africa.

probably quite painful and it must be left feeling quite sore; at best, it is left with a tell-tale circular scar, and at worst, its wound could become infected.

There are two potential food items that most sharks generally seem to ignore: decaying flesh of their own kind, and jellyfish. Consisting mostly of water, jellyfish are not noted for their protein or fat content, although blacktip reef sharks, bronze whalers and a handful of other species do occasionally eat them – perhaps when there is little else around.

When they are hunting, sharks instinctively assess the value of a potential prey item. Is it likely to provide enough nourishment to justify the energy needed to chase and catch it? This is why most sharks tend to ignore healthy, fully grown prey animals, which have a good chance of escape. They prefer to tackle easier prey – youngsters, ill or injured adults, or even dead animals. One argument for shark conservation is that in this way they provide a critical service by weeding out unfit and poorly adapted individuals from their prey populations.

Digestive system

Sharks lack both the jaw musculature and the molars that would enable them to chew their food. They swallow smaller prey whole, or bite off and swallow small chunks of larger prey (which are torn away with a vigorous shaking of the head until the teeth have sliced through the flesh and bone).

Sharks have a powerful digestive system, capable of breaking down these lumps of food into molecule-sized pieces that can be absorbed from the gut into the body. But it does normally take a long time. Most sharks digest their food relatively slowly, often over several days. This is partly because most of them are cold-blooded – their body temperatures vary with the temperature of the surrounding water – and the colder the surroundings, the longer digestion takes. The sophisticated modification of the circulatory system that effectively makes the great white, thresher sharks and a handful of others warm-blooded results in much faster digestion in these few species. The higher temperature increases the activity of the digestive

enzymes, enabling the sharks to feed again rapidly should the opportunity arise. A warm-blooded shortfin mako can digest a meal in a day or a little longer, but a cold-blooded sandbar shark takes three days or more to digest a similar amount of food.

The shark's digestive tract is basically a long tube, with some parts wider than others, that stretches from the mouth to the cloaca (the rear chamber into which the digestive tract empties). It is relatively short compared to the digestive tract of humans and other vertebrates.

A slimy mucous in the mouth eases the passage of food into the throat, and then muscle contractions force it along the short, narrow gullet, or oesophagus. It enters the stomach, where it is attacked by strong digestive juices, acids and enzymes for hours or even days. The stomach is large, stretchy and expandable and capable of storing huge quantities of food. This is especially important for ocean wanderers, such as oceanic whitetip sharks, because their prey is sparse and they often have huge meals with long gaps in between.

The stomach produces a soupy mush, which enters the intestines via two key structures: the pyloric sphincter and then the spiral valve. The pyloric sphincter is basically a ring of muscle that contracts and relaxes at intervals to allow the semi-digested food to dribble into the intestines at a steady rate. It also serves as a screening device between the stomach and intestines to filter out bones, shells and any other troublesome bits and pieces that are difficult or impossible to digest. When enough of this unwanted matter has collected at the pyloric sphincter, it is regurgitated by turning the stomach inside-out. The stomach literally emerges from the shark's mouth like an inverted balloon until all the unwanted indigestible matter has been jettisoned into the sea. The end result is akin to vomiting in humans, or owls

Opposite: A shark can turn its stomach inside-out (so it emerges from the mouth) to jettison all unwanted indigestible matter into the sea.

regurgitating pellets of indigestible fur and feathers. Everting the stomach is also a means of defence. The cloud of unwanted food washed into the water helps to distract a predator with its eye on the shark, and may even provide an alternative meal (albeit second-best to the shark itself). Unfortunately, sharks often evert their stomachs when they are caught, and, perhaps not surprisingly, they are killed by fishermen believing it to be the humane thing to do. But sharks quickly re-absorb the stomach and may be none the worse for their experience if released.

The corkscrew-like spiral valve is unique to sharks. It effectively replaces the very long intestines found in most other vertebrates, and is designed to increase the surface area for maximum absorption of nutrients (our intestines are looped and coiled for the same purpose). The design of the spiral valve varies from species to species. In the pelagic thresher, for instance, it is shaped rather like a spiral staircase, while in the dusky shark it is scroll-shaped. As the semi-solid waste material passes through the valve into the rectum, it takes on its unique shape, so each shark species has its own characteristic faeces.

The downside of the spiral valve is that it is a favourite lodging site for internal parasites – particularly tapeworms. The spiral valve of a single blue shark may be home to more than 1000 tapeworms, and the smooth dogfish has a different species of tapeworm in each of the first four chambers of its spiral valve; by the time food reaches the fifth chamber (there are eight altogether), too many of the nutrients have been removed for another tapeworm to bother setting up home.

Migrations

Some sharks never venture far from their small home patch, but others travel vast distances between continents in their constant search for food. There are non-migratory species, such as bull sharks, nurse sharks and bonnetheads, which are usually found near shore or around coral reefs, and rarely travel more than a few hundred kilometres. For instance, the famous bull sharks of Walker's Cay in the Bahamas are present all year round, except for June and July, when they follow the tuna migration for a couple of months. Then there are sharks that are capable of migrating 1600 km (1000 miles) or more, but normally stay in deep waters over the continental shelf; these include tiger sharks, blacktip sharks and sandbar sharks. And there are the really great travellers, including blue sharks and shortfin makos, which make long, often intercontinental, migrations across deep ocean basins.

Many species follow the movements of their prey, so their migrations are seasonal. Some associate with other animals that feed on the same prey. Oceanic whitetip sharks, for instance, travel with pods of short-finned pilot whales, perhaps taking advantage of the pilots' remarkable ability to find squid by echolocation, or even feeding on the whales when they become injured or ill.

Predators of sharks

Sharks are not immune to predation themselves. Even the great white shark – the ultimate predator, and probably the most feared creature on the planet – is not entirely safe. A few years ago a killer whale was observed catching and killing a 3-m (10-feet) great white at the Farallon Islands, off the coast of California.

The sheer size of larger species – even inoffensive basking sharks and whale sharks – gives them some degree of protection. They are simply too big for most predators to tackle. But juveniles are susceptible to a wide range of predators. They fall prey to everything from crocodiles to seals, and are hunted by many types of larger sharks. Their main defence is to hide. Lemon sharks, for instance, are born in shallow bays and lagoons, well out of harm's way. They spend their first two years skulking around in the seaweed and mangrove roots and staying as far away from other

sharks – including their own parents – as they possibly can. As they grow older, and bigger, they are in less danger of being eaten, and can begin to creep out into deeper water.

Providing a free meal

Despite their ravenous reputations, sharks have surprisingly friendly associations with several other fishes – even ones that are roughly the same size as their normal prey.

Pilot fish (so called by the Ancient Greeks, who believed they could guide ships to land), are ocean-going bony fishes, found mainly in sub-tropical waters, which frequently travel with sharks. Typically about 1 m (40 inches) in length, they may take advantage of their hosts' messy eating habits and feast on the scraps scattered in the water after a kill (although recent studies have revealed the stomach contents of pilot fish to be whole small fishes, not leftover scraps, so there is some uncertainty about what they do eat). They also gain a degree of protection – after all, where is safer than alongside the business end of a shark? (Other fishes sometimes crowd around sharks for protection: off Cape Hatteras, on the east coast of the USA, large sand tiger sharks are often surrounded by clouds of small fish seeking protection from passing amberjacks and barracuda.) The pilot fish may also conserve energy by hitching a ride in the shark's slipstream. It is uncertain how the sharks benefit from this arrangement, but one possibility is that the pilot fish – which are indiscriminate feeders – also dine on the sharks' parasites, and therefore help to keep them fit and healthy.

Whale sharks have their own part-time pilot fish. They are often accompanied by distinctive black-and-yellow-striped fishes, which swim just in front of their enormous, broad mouths. These

Opposite: A whale shark with its entourage of remoras in the Sea of Cortez, Mexico.

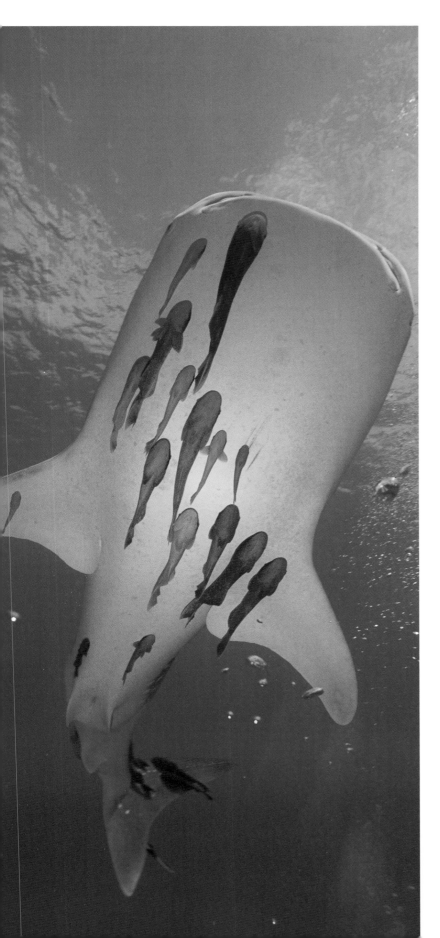

are young golden trevally, which stay with the whale sharks until they are mature, and then, when they lose their stripes, take their leave to join large shoals of their contemporaries.

Remoras, or sharksuckers, literally attach themselves to the sharks with the help of modified dorsal fins that form special oval suckers on the top of their heads. There is a powerful vacuum between the sucker and the shark, enabling the slim fishes to cling on with a force that would support at least 10 kg (22 lb). They ride the oceans for free, no matter how fast their predatory hosts are swimming. There are three main species (*Remora remora*, *Echeneis naucrates* and *Remorina albescens*), ranging from about 20 cm (8 inches) to nearly 1 m (40 inches) in length. They feed on their host's other parasites, including copepods and isopods (fish lice), and clean up the scraps after a meal. In the Bahamas, sharksuckers even gather on pregnant lemon sharks as they approach full term, and, when the pups are born, not only eat the afterbirth, but may also assist by breaking and eating the umbilical cord.

Other fishes wait at 'cleaning stations', where sharks queue up for a professional manicure, and some even dare to feed around the predators' mouths. The cleaners get an easy meal and a guarantee of safety, in return for removing all their customers' parasites. The cleaners are finger-sized wrasse, which are common inhabitants of coral reefs in many parts of the world. They wander over the bodies and enter the mouths and gill slits of visiting sharks (as well as barracudas, groupers, manta rays and a variety of other fearsome giants) to pick off dead skin and scar tissue, scraps of food, barnacles, fungi and any other debris. Most importantly, they pick off nasty parasites – which they consider to be a delicacy – and may therefore play an important role in preventing diseases from being transmitted. No one knows how the cleaners get away with such daring behaviour, although they do have distinct patterns and dances, which may inhibit the killer instinct of their clients.

Shark Attacks in Perspective

Fear Distorts the Facts

Sharks have probably had a bad press since people first started talking and writing. Just imagine the tales told, embellished and retold by our ancestors sitting around their campfires overlooking the sea. They probably did not notice the vast majority of sharks, inoffensively going about their business out of sight and out of mind, but they would certainly have heard about the small minority that inflicted terrible injuries on their fellow sailors and fishermen. And, of course, there is little doubt that shark attack stories are far more attention-grabbing than attacks by other animals that bite people far more frequently.

One of the first shark attacks recorded in detail took place in 1580, when a sailor fell overboard during a voyage from Portugal to India. He was thrown a rope, but, as members of the crew began to haul him back towards the ship, a large shark appeared from nowhere and tore the poor man apart before he could be hauled aboard. A more famous attack happened nearly two centuries later, in 1749, when Brooks Watson, who later became Lord Mayor of London, had one of his legs bitten off by a shark.

But the risk of shark attack did not really become a significant fear in the public mind until the twentieth century. The Second World War was a major turning-point, when servicemen from shipwrecks and downed planes were suddenly thrown into 'shark-infested waters'. The USS *Indianapolis* is a classic example of the havoc wreaked by sharks during some of these wartime disasters. The warship had been to Guam, delivering components of the atomic bomb later dropped on Hiroshima, and was bound for the Philippines. There were 1199 men on board when, at midnight on 30 July 1945, the ship was torpedoed by a Japanese submarine. There was no time to put lifeboats into the water – the

stricken vessel sank in just 12 minutes – and the sailors had to leap for their lives. More than 900 managed to get off the ship alive: some wore lifejackets, others were left clinging to the wreckage. Almost immediately, sharks came to investigate. Eyewitness accounts suggest that they may have been oceanic whitetips, but this has never been verified, and there could have been other species there as well. The men could see the sharks circling in the clear water below for several frightening days. Then, one night, there were anguished screams as the sharks began to move in for the kill, and from then on most of the sailors were eaten in front of their shipmates. By the time rescuers arrived on 8 August (no one had raised the alarm because of the clandestine nature of the ship's mission) there were just 316 survivors.

Publicized to death

In recent years, a more cosmopolitan news-gathering system and a greater demand for shocking and titillating stories are partly to blame for our obsession with sharks: a headline reading 'Shark

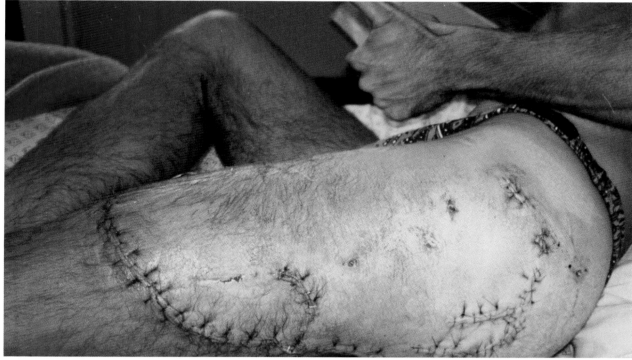

Page 90: A great white shark – one of the most feared, maligned and misunderstood creatures on the planet.

Opposite: Hundreds of men were taken by sharks when the USS *Indianapolis* was torpedoed and sunk in 1945.

Right: Recovering in hospital after a serious shark attack in 1995.

Attacks Man' sells newspapers and does little to curtail our fear of them. Another contributing factor is the growing amount of time that people spend by the sea. In the USA, for instance, the past 25 years or so has witnessed a mass rush for the seashore; more than half the population of 280 million people now lives within 80 km (50 miles) of the sea. Many others visit for short periods. Perhaps inevitably, when so many people are spending so much time in the sea, they take a personal interest in what might be lurking in the hidden depths.

At least some of the blame must rest with the book *Jaws*, published in 1974, and with the high-profile movies that followed. They literally scared audiences out of the water, and many shark conservationists believe they were largely responsible for the anti-shark hysteria that has gripped the Western world ever since. Even the book's author, Peter Benchley, publicly laments the impact of his book on our attitude towards sharks, and is now actively involved in shark conservation.

In the days when *Jaws* was published, many experts were just as unenlightened. Until surprisingly recently, diving

magazines and books used to suggest that the only sensible thing to do if a shark appeared was to leave the water. The mere hint of sharks at a diving resort was enough to drive tourists away and threaten the livelihoods of the local operators.

Now we know better. Statistically, even if you spend a great deal of time in the sea, the likelihood of being attacked by a shark is ridiculously small. Here are a few revealing comparisons to put the risk into perspective: there is a far greater chance of winning a national lottery than of being attacked by a shark; more than six times as many people are struck by lightning every year in Florida (which is the world's shark-attack hotspot) than are attacked by sharks; around the world 1000 people drown for every one person attacked by a shark; many times more people are killed by coconuts falling on their heads than are killed by sharks; and, best of all, according to figures published by the New York City Health Department, for every person around the world bitten by a shark, 25 people are actually bitten by New Yorkers. Perhaps the most shocking statistic – and this really puts things into perspective – is that in an average year for every person killed by

a shark, we in turn kill many *millions* of sharks. Now that really is frightening. There are many more weird and wonderful facts and figures, some more meaningful than others, but they all add up to one thing: sharks are not intent on hurting people at all.

Unfortunately, statistics offer little comfort to the unfortunate few who *are* attacked by sharks and, given the fear and anxiety fuelled by the movie industry and the popular press, it is not surprising that the rest of us take little reassurance from the truth. Yet few of us will ever encounter a real, live shark in the wild, and even fewer will be threatened, much less harmed, by one. Perhaps our fear of sharks is so deep that it stems from a subconscious fear of the unknown and the unexpected? Or perhaps we feel profoundly unsettled by the shark's robotic stare, giving the impression that it is without feeling, compassion or

reason? Harvard biologist E. O. Wilson believes that our endless fascination with predators of any kind is a survival strategy: 'We're not just afraid of predators, we're transfixed by them...because fascination creates preparedness, and preparedness, survival.'

Most shark experts are as keen to survive as we all are, but whenever they enter the water, they are probably more rational in their fear. No one in their right mind would go on safari and waltz around with a pride of lions, yet, in theory, that is precisely the risk many researchers are taking during the course of their work. But they enter the water with humility and understanding. That is not to say that they have become cavalier, though. There is a huge difference between being afraid of sharks and being cautiously respectful of them.

The 'Summer of the Shark'

Unfortunately fear, not respect, is what makes news. And the summer of 2001 was when our fear of sharks reached an all-time high as a direct result of a media feeding frenzy that has not been seen before or since.

It began at dusk on 6 July 2001, when eight-year-old Jesse Arborgast lost an arm and a third of one thigh during an attack by a 2.1-m (7-feet) bull shark in shallow water off Pensacola, Florida. His quick-thinking uncle somehow managed to wrestle the shark ashore and, with the help of a park ranger, retrieved Jesse's severed arm from its mouth. Although he survived, and doctors even managed to reattach his arm, Jesse is still struggling to cope with his terrible injuries. *Time* magazine proclaimed it the 'Summer of the Shark' on the cover of its 30 July issue. Then, on Labor Day weekend that September, a ten-year-old boy was killed by a shark at Virginia Beach in Virginia, and a 28-year-old man was killed in North Carolina. From then on shark attacks were a major news item, until 11 September, when the focus moved to international issues.

Very quickly, the world had been led to believe that 2001 was an exceptional year for shark attacks and the press kept count of the supposed carnage taking place, particularly along the east coast of the USA. Self-proclaimed experts came up with various theories to explain the non-existent problem, ranging from a lack of fish prey to a population explosion of bull sharks. There was even a story claiming that Fidel Castro had concocted a scheme to breed dangerous sharks and unleash them on an unsuspecting American public (and on Cuban rafters). As Peter Benchley, the author of *Jaws*, commented: 'Never before, to my knowledge, has so much ink and so much airtime been devoted

to so few events of little national or international consequence.'

The 'Summer of the Shark' story was complete fiction. The facts prove that the hysteria was completely unjustified and there was no summer of the shark. By US standards, 2001 was an average year; by international standards, it was actually below average. Around the world, the number of unprovoked shark attacks recorded in 2001 was 72, down from 85 the previous year; the number of serious attacks was down, too: there were five fatalities in 2001, and 13 the year before. In the USA, the number of unprovoked attacks was 53 in 2001 – exactly one fewer than in 2000. Many more statistics, based on data recorded over many years, support the expert view that 2001 was a fairly normal year. What should have made the headlines, perhaps, was the fact that 4000 people drowned in 2001, in the USA alone. It really puts the shark attacks into perspective. But even if 2001 had been an exceptional year with a record number of shark attacks, experts do not assign too much significance to year-to-year variability. They view short-term trends – up or down – with a certain amount of caution. There are simply too many variables, from the weather to the economic climate, that can influence the local abundance of sharks and the number of people in the water (and therefore the odds of an attack).

Another noteworthy attack made headline news the following year, in April 2002, when behavioural ecologist and shark researcher Erich Ritter was attacked by a bull shark while being interviewed for a television programme on Walker's Cay in the Bahamas. A rather unorthodox researcher, who had previously claimed that he protected himself from shark attack by using yoga techniques to make himself calm and confident, Ritter lost a large chunk of his leg when the shark bit deep into his calf. Bull sharks are considered by many to be the most dangerous sharks of all, and yet Ritter was standing with bare legs in waist-deep water that was heavily baited with pieces of fish, and he was literally surrounded by large adult sharks. Ritter laid his life on

Opposite: In an average year more people are attacked by sharks here, at New Smyrna Beach, Florida, than at any other single location in the world.

the line to prove his theory that, like dogs, sharks can detect fear in people and this triggers the attack response. But in those murky shallows, it seems that one of the sharks mistook his pale-coloured leg for a fish. Other shark researchers believe that the attack was a grim inevitability and are rather concerned that it has had a negative impact on our view of sharks and shark attack.

The International Shark Attack File

The primary source of information on shark attack is the International Shark Attack File (ISAF), which is a detailed compilation of all known shark attacks around the world from the mid-1500s to the present day. Established in 1958, following a conference involving scientists from 34 nations concerned about the lack of dependable information on shark attack, the file is owned by the Smithsonian Institution, administered by the American Elasmobranch Society and housed at the Florida Museum of Natural History.

More than 3550 individual investigations are currently held in the ISAF, of which 2154 have been confirmed as unprovoked shark attacks. Approximately 26 per cent (544 attacks) of these proved fatal. Information on each attack is screened and computerized, but the database also includes a permanent archive of all the associated material, from original notes and press clippings to videotapes and medical or autopsy reports.

How many people are attacked?

Worldwide there are probably 70–100 shark attacks every year, on average, resulting in about 5–15 deaths. The figures are a little vague because not all shark attacks are reported, especially in the developing world and in parts of the West where, even these days, some attacks are intentionally kept quiet for fear of adverse publicity.

The number of unprovoked shark attacks has grown at a steady rate over the past century. Overall, there were more confirmed 'unprovoked' attacks (522) during the 1990s than during any previous decade on record, and the 2000–2002 totals continue that upward trend. There were more attacks in 2000 (85) than in any year since shark attack statistics were first recorded by ISAF. But this does not reflect a change in the per capita rate of attack and does not mean that sharks are getting more dangerous. There are simply many more people in the sea these days – swimming, snorkelling, diving, surfing and spearfishing – so more attacks are to be expected. Also, the scientific network and techniques used to discover, investigate and file shark attacks have improved enormously in recent years. In the past decade in particular, a greater interest in shark attacks worldwide, coupled with the ISAF's strong web presence, has resulted in many shark attacks being reported that could easily have been missed in the past.

By contrast, the death rate has declined. Fewer people die from shark attack these days than they did in the past. Again, this has nothing to do with the number or severity of attacks, but reflects the advent of readily available emergency services and a dramatic improvement in the quality of medical treatment.

In 2002, the latest year for which complete figures are available, the ISAF investigated 86 alleged incidents of shark attacks around the world. It was concluded that 60 of them involved genuine unprovoked attacks (in other words, 60 people were attacked by wild sharks in their natural habitats without provocation). This total is comparable with previous years – slightly lower than for 2001 (72) and 2000 (85) – and slightly higher than 1999 (58) and 1998 (54). The 26 attacks not accorded unprovoked status in 2002 included: 14 provoked attacks (mostly involving divers or fishermen handling sharks), three attacks on boats, three dismissed as non-attacks, and six with insufficient information. Shark-inflicted damage to people who were already dead (normally drowned) and interactions between sharks and divers in public aquariums or research tanks are not considered to be attacks, and are not included in these statistics. There were three fatalities during the year: two in Australia and one in Brazil. This is a significantly lower fatality rate (5 per cent) than the average for the 1990s (13 per cent).

There are a number of possible reasons for a relatively small number of shark attacks in certain years (apart from chance). These include: a weak economy (meaning that fewer people can afford to visit beaches), poor weather (which deters them from entering the sea once they are there), and overfishing (resulting in fewer sharks or fewer bait fish).

Even the highest attack incidence – 85 in 2000 – is minuscule considering the millions of people in the sea around the world every day. Just imagine the number of human–shark encounters that take place in Hawaii, for instance, where the beaches are filled with bathers and surfers, and where tiger sharks could almost be described as common. Most people in the water would have no idea if they have had a close encounter with a tiger shark, but there is no doubt that the shark would have known. It is clear that if sharks were deliberately hunting people, there would be many more attacks.

Below: There are so many people paddling, swimming, snorkelling, surfing and diving in the sea around the world every day that there would be many more attacks if sharks really were out to get us.

What provokes a shark to attack?

Why sharks attack people is a subject of endless, and often heated, debate. There are no simple answers: sharks have been known to attack for many different reasons and, on occasion, for no apparent reason.

The traditional view is that there are two main types of shark attack: provoked, when someone deliberately annoys the shark by pulling on its tail for instance, and unprovoked, when the person has done nothing to make it angry. But it could be argued that there is no such thing as an unprovoked attack on the basis that the shark itself probably has a very good reason for attacking even if it is not immediately obvious to the victim. In a way, we provoke sharks merely by entering the water with them, by moving into their space.

Given the chance, a few large sharks *will* eat people, and there are occasional stories of sharks that develop a taste for human flesh in the same way that certain lions and tigers become man-eaters. For instance, there was an attack on three people in Queensland, Australia, when their boat sank in 1983, and they were methodically picked off one by one by the same shark. However, no shark species actually appears to favour the taste of human flesh. Most do not seem even to *like* the way we taste. Lacking hands to explore things, they use their mouths instead, but since their limits are very different from our own, even a single exploratory bite can prove fatal. Such attacks are normally unprovoked, although if the victim is distressed or injured (perhaps after an aircraft or ship disaster), the sharks may be stimulated to attack.

Some researchers studying great white sharks believe that they bite unfamiliar objects to test them as a potential food source, and if those objects – like humans and surfboards – have a low fat content, they are rejected. Even the most overweight person would be insufficiently fat to satisfy a hungry great white, which may be why most people are bitten once and then spat out. It would take a large shark several days to digest a human, and meanwhile it could be feeding much more productively on a calorie-rich seal or tuna. Other researchers believe that great whites make an initial strike, then release their prey and retreat a safe distance away from its potentially harmful jaws and teeth until it has bled to death. Recent research in South Africa does not support this bite-and-wait theory, but it has been observed in California, and might be a local adaptation to tackling large and powerful bull elephant seals.

Even if a shark has no intention of eating you, or tasting you, it may still bite in self-defence. Many animals will bite if they feel threatened, and sharks are no exception. Species that are normally quite docile can, quite understandably, react aggressively if they feel harrassed. Nurse sharks, for instance, are generally considered harmless: they feed mainly at night, on bottom-dwelling invertebrates, and spend most of the day asleep. But some divers cannot resist the urge to grab their dorsal fins for a free ride, or to pull their tails when they find them sticking out of a cave or from underneath a ledge. The result is fairly predictable – the shark takes a defensive bite and rapidly swims away. To be fair to the sharks, such injuries should be attributed to defence rather than attack.

The risk of attack may also be increased by luring the sharks with food. This is particularly true if they are denied access to the food once they have arrived on the scene. Some experts consider spearfishing, for example, to be the underwater equivalent of drink-driving: in other words, it is asking for trouble. It results in low-frequency, erratic vibrations of distressed fishes (because they are not killed outright), which are highly attractive to sharks and can result in a confrontation.

Another possible reason for attack is personal space. A person inadvertently wandering into a shark's space may receive

Opposite: Is this windsurfer in danger? Probably not, according to international shark attack statistics.

an aggressive social warning, typically resulting in a slash wound similar to those found on the sharks themselves. There are numerous examples where sharks have apparently attempted to force divers away from 'their' area (which could be a radius of 10 m (33 feet) or more around the sharks, but varies from species to species and from individual to individual).

Types of attack

The ISAF identifies three distinct kinds of unprovoked shark attack: 'hit-and-run', 'bump-and-bite', and 'sneak' attacks.

Hit-and-run attacks are by far the most common. The victims are normally swimmers or surfers in the surf zone, who seldom see their attacker and get bitten only once. Most of the bites are on the leg, typically below the knee, and are rarely life-threatening. These attacks are probably cases of mistaken identity. The shark attacks once, then realizes its error and swims away. Imagine the scenario: a hunting shark in poor water visibility and in a harsh environment with breaking surf; add a person splashing about, perhaps wearing shiny jewellery, a brightly coloured swimsuit or wetsuit, and with uneven tanning (especially white soles of the feet). What is surprising is that, under these conditions, sharks do not misinterpret human limbs for their normal prey more often.

Bump-and-bite attacks are less common, but more dangerous. The victims are normally swimmers or divers in deeper water, and, typically, the sharks circle and bump them prior to the actual attack. When they do bump, their abrasive skin causes wounds, which spill blood into the water, and it is this that can trigger a shark's instinct to feed.

Sneak attacks are as dangerous as bump-and-bite attacks, but normally occur without warning. In both cases, the sharks will often attack repeatedly and multiple injuries are the norm. Most fatalities occur as a result of these two forms of attack, which are unlikely to be cases of mistaken identity, since the sharks are probably actively feeding or defending their personal space. It is the classic attack pattern of the ocean's top killers, such as the great white, tiger, bull and oceanic whitetip.

Where are the shark attack hotspots?

Shark attacks can occur almost anywhere and under any circumstances: in murky water or clear, rough water or calm, good weather or bad, warm water or cold, low tide or high, and during the day or at night. But there do seem to be certain trends. Most attacks occur close to the shore, in water between knee-deep and chin-deep, and many are in the water between the mainland and a sandbar. Areas with steep drop-offs, where sharks congregate to hunt their natural prey, are also common attack sites.

The 522 unprovoked shark attacks recorded worldwide during the 1990s were centred on surprisingly few locations: Florida (185), South Africa (55), Brazil (49), Hawaii (33), Australia (28), California (26), New Zealand (17) and the rest of the world (129).

As in most years, the vast majority of attacks in 2002 occurred in the USA. In fact, the USA accounted for no less than 78 per cent of all shark attacks (47 out of 60). The actual number of attacks was slightly down on previous years (53 in 2001 and 54 in 2000); the percentage on a world scale was similar to 2001 (74 per cent) and slightly up on 2000 (64 per cent). Six attacks were recorded in Hawaii, four in California, three in North Carolina, two in South Carolina, one in Oregon and one in Texas; another attack occurred offshore in the Gulf of Mexico.

Florida usually accounts for the majority of attacks in the USA, and the past three years have been no exception: 29 in 2002, 37 in 2001, and 38 in 2000. This makes Florida *the* world shark attack hotspot. There are several possible reasons why it

Right: Not for the faint-hearted: a diver enjoys a thrilling close encounter with a great white shark.

has such a high incidence of shark attack: it has 2054 km (1277 miles) of coastline, it is home to many potentially dangerous species of sharks, and there are huge numbers of people (residents and tourists) in the water at any one time. At least 14 different shark species have been implicated in the attacks, but the five main culprits are believed to be blacktip sharks, bull sharks, spinner sharks, nurse sharks and hammerheads. Within Florida, Volusia County usually has more attacks than anywhere else (18 in 2002 and 22 in 2001), and one particular site, New Smyrna Beach, is the record-holder. Some 10–15 surfers are bitten here in an average year and there were no fewer than six attacks over a single weekend in August 2001.

Who do sharks attack?

Men are attacked by sharks more often than women. Studies of shark attacks on divers in recent years reveal that approximately ten times as many men are attacked as women. This is not because sharks actively select men rather than women, but probably because there tend to be more men in the sea, and they have a habit of swimming or surfing alone in deep water more often than women. Similarly, most divers attacked by sharks are 20–40 years old, simply because that is the age range most commonly involved in diving.

More than half (56 per cent) of the attacks during 2002 were on surfers, and it is probably no coincidence that most shark-attack hotspots around the world are also major surf centres. There were 32 incidents during the year altogether. Nearly a third of all the world's shark attacks in 2002 (18 out of 60) were at an

inlet near New Smyrna Beach, in Florida, which is a popular surfing site. There has been a phenomenal increase in the popularity of surfing since the early 1950s, and surfers spend much longer in the sea than swimmers, and venture farther offshore. Traditional theory suggests that a large shark can easily mistake a surfer on a surfboard for its natural prey because the silhouette looks remarkably like an elephant seal or sea lion when viewed from below, although some experts doubt this as a plausible explanation. This may be true in some cases, but it is more likely that a smaller shark might mistake the soles of the feet and palms of the hands, which tend to be much lighter than the rest of the surfer's wetsuit or tanned skin, for the flashing white of fish.

Swimmers and paddlers were the next most frequent victims – with 22 incidents accounting for about a third (34 per cent) of the 2002 attacks – followed by divers and snorkellers with just four attacks (7 per cent). Attacks on divers and snorkellers are surprisingly rare. In the past 20 years, just over 5 per cent of all

Right, centre and far right: Seen from below, a surfer on a surfboard creates a silhouette that some experts believe could be mistaken for a sea lion or a sea turtle, the natural prey of some large sharks.

the world's unprovoked shark attacks have been on scuba-divers, and approximately 14 per cent on snorkellers. A diver under water usually attracts less interest from a shark than a snorkeller or swimmer on the surface. Indeed, many people who have happily been diving with sharks for years do not feel comfortable swimming on the surface, especially in deep water, without a mask, snorkel and fins.

It is imperative for swimmers to know if sharks are present and what they are doing. If they do appear, it may not be necessary to leave the water, but at least it is possible to make an informed decision. Divers participating in organized shark dives are by no means immune to attack, although in these instances human error of judgement is usually a contributory factor. Even during cage dives, people have been bitten on their hands when they have placed them outside the cage to take photographs or to try and touch passing sharks. In recent years, more than a dozen injuries have occurred during organized

shark feeds, although most of the victims were people running the events.

Whether diving or snorkelling, spearfishing undoubtedly increases the chance of a shark encounter. According to ISAF statistics, a significant number of victims were spearfishing or carrying fish at the time of attack. Spearfishing on an outgoing tide is probably more dangerous than on an incoming tide because there are more sharks offshore and they tend to be larger, more dangerous species. But whatever the tide, trailing fish juices and swimming erratically is a sure way of attracting hungry sharks.

The most dangerous sharks

In the majority of shark attacks, it is difficult to identify the species responsible. In particular, very little is known about those involved in hit-and-run attacks because they are seldom seen. Even with more prolonged bump-and-bite and sneak attacks, few

victims are able to make a positive identification, and their wounds rarely provide sufficient clues for experts to do it for them.

By their very nature, no sharks are actually friendly. Most of them are, however, surprisingly placid in the company of people, and the two largest – the whale shark and the basking shark – have a positively mellow disposition. Nevertheless, the ISAF has been able to implicate no fewer than 42 shark species in a total of 980 attacks over the past 420 years (1580–2000).

According to these statistics, three species accounted for more than half of all attacks:

▼   Great white shark – responsible for 254 unprovoked attacks on people (67 of which were fatal), as well as 14 provoked attacks and 64 attacks on boats. A further 25 incidents were reported with insufficient information.

▼   Tiger shark – responsible for 91 unprovoked attacks on people (29 of which were fatal), as well as seven provoked attacks and nine attacks on boats. A further 25 incidents were reported with insufficient information.

▼   Bull shark – responsible for 66 unprovoked attacks on people (20 of which were fatal), as well as 11 provoked attacks and four attacks on boats. A further five incidents were reported with insufficient information.

The findings are not particularly surprising, since these are all large, widely distributed sharks, and are capable of tackling sizeable prey. Despite the figures, the bull shark is considered by some authorities to be the most dangerous of all sharks, and it is possible that some (or many) of the attacks attributed to great whites and tiger sharks could be the work of these heavy-bodied, powerful predators. But any shark longer than about 1.8 m (6 feet) is potentially dangerous to people and should be treated with extra caution.

Several other species were responsible for a significant number of unprovoked attacks on people over the same period, including the following:

▼   Sand tiger shark – 37 (including one fatality)

▼   Blacktip shark – 28 (with no fatalities)

▼   Hammerhead shark – 19 (with no fatalities)

▼   Blue shark – 14 (including three fatalities)

The list of attackers also includes some rather unlikely species, such as the cookie-cutter shark, the spiny dogfish and the Ganges shark, although in these particular cases there is just one incident attributed to each species. The youngest shark to bite a human was an unborn sand tiger pup, which bit a marine biologist while he was examining the uterus of its dead mother. Every shark should therefore be treated with respect.

How not to become a statistic

According to all the available data, the frequency and pattern of shark attacks on people has less to do with the behaviour of the sharks and more to do with the behaviour of people in the water. At one time, for example, it was believed that sharks rarely attack in water colder than 20°C (70°F). In a way, this is true, but it is because people are reluctant to go into the water when it is too cold, so there are fewer human–shark encounters. As the number of people in the water increases, there are more opportunities for a shark to attack. It is therefore helpful to be aware of the kind of human behaviour that makes sharks forget their manners.

For divers and snorkellers, there are basically two golden rules for reducing the risk of shark attack: never underestimate the shark, and never overestimate your abilities or knowledge as a diver or snorkeller. Remember that nearly all dangers arise from inexperience or misjudgement of a situation. Inevitably, the more time you spend with sharks, the better you become at identifying different species – which in turn helps to make a preliminary assessment of the potential threat – and the better you become at understanding their unspoken language.

But predicting and interpreting shark behaviour is not as simple as it may sound because all sharks behave differently, and, like humans, can have bad days and act out of character. So, faced with a fast-swimming shark rushing straight towards you, there may be no way of telling whether it is going to attack or veer off at the last moment. As Jacques Cousteau once commented, the only predictable thing about sharks is that they are unpredictable. There are, however, certain warning signs that make it possible to predict a possible attack, or at least to recognize an unhappy shark. These are more marked in some species than others, but include swimming fast or jerkily, swimming in a tight figure of

Opposite: The tiger shark is considered one of the world's most dangerous sharks, but many divers have encountered this large predator without incident.

eight or tight circles, contorting the body into a distinctive S-shape, arching the back, pushing the pectoral fins downwards, lifting the snout, swinging the head from side to side, and jaw-gaping. These ritualized displays work, in some species, as warnings, and may precede a direct attack. The shark is shouting 'Get out of here!' and quite obviously looks and acts agitated. Every other animal in the water recognizes the message – and it is important for divers and snorkellers to recognize it too.

Avoiding a shark attack is not a precise science, of course, but there are some interesting factors to bear in mind:

▼ Check for telltale signs before you enter the water. Take a moment to look at the sea around you in case there are signs that sharks might be lurking underneath. If there is a disturbance anywhere in an otherwise calm sea, do not go into the water. Similarly, if there are seabirds swooping and diving, ripples on the water, or silvery flashes of tiny scales, sharks could be driving bait fish up towards the surface.

▼ Think about what you are wearing. Some sharks may be able to tell one colour from another, and many can distinguish light colours from dark. There is some evidence to suggest that bright colours, such as white and silver, may attract them and, rightly or wrongly, 'yum-yum yellow' has a particularly bad reputation. It is not unusual for sharks to bite at light-coloured fins (perhaps because they look like separate small fish), at the glint of light on face-masks and camera lenses, or at shiny jewellery (which may resemble fish scales). Uneven tanning may have a similar effect. According to ISAF statistics, 60 per cent of divers and snorkellers attacked were wearing highly contrasting colours, very bright colours, or shiny items, such as jewellery. Although such statistics are difficult to evaluate without analysing the popularity of different colours and jewellery among water-users, some experts do prefer to wear dull-coloured clothing and equipment.

▼ Do not make too much noise. Unusual or irregular sounds definitely attract sharks, often from a long distance away. All erratic movements send out a signal that says 'Wounded prey... worth investigating'. Sharks will also investigate the impact of an aircraft plunging into the sea, or even of a person diving in from a boat. Irregular movements, such as those made by a swimmer in trouble or merely splashing about for fun, can be another attractant. Do not even swim in the sea with a dog because dogs swim with an erratic, ungainly motion that can attract the attention of curious sharks.

▼ Check that you are not bleeding. Traces of blood may attract some species of shark. So do other body fluids, such as vomit and urine.

▼ Try not to be alone in the water. Sharks are more likely to attack a solitary individual or someone separated from other members of a group. As a lone swimmer – even if you are just a short distance from everyone else – you are vulnerable prey.

▼ Be careful where you swim. Do not go swimming in areas where sharks are likely to congregate, such as steep drop-offs, narrow passes into tropical lagoons, and channels into harbours; and do not enter the water when there are likely to be unusually high numbers of sharks around, such as during the sardine run in South Africa. Swimming in murky water also increases the risk of shark attack because it is more difficult for the sharks to distinguish between your limbs (which might appear to be separate animals) and their natural prey. And do not swim where people are fishing from boats – they may have baited the water with blood, guts and fish bits that sharks are sure to investigate.

▼ Do not go swimming at dusk, dawn or at night. Some sharks are believed to feed at twilight, so the risk of an attack may increase substantially if you are in the water early in the morning or late in the afternoon – and, of course, they can see you, while you probably cannot see them. The same sharks that are timid and unapproachable during the day may be more inquisitive at dusk and dawn. In addition, more dangerous sharks may move into shallower water at night. In some parts of the world tiger sharks, for example, often come into the shallows after dark to feed.

▼ Be cautious when swimming with marine mammals. Many shark species accompany or hunt seals, dolphins and other marine mammals. Anyone tempted to swim with them should be alert to the very real possibility that they may be accompanied by sharks. Playful pinnipeds, for example, are the favourite prey of great white sharks and some other large species. These sharks can be aggressive, perhaps because human intruders are seen as an easy meal or unwanted competition. Certainly never swim with marine mammals without wearing a mask, snorkel and fins, which ensure that you swim smoothly without too much splashing and enable you to see if sharks are present. It is also advisable to wear a wetsuit, which provides some protection if the sharks bump you. Sea turtles also fall prey to sharks – most notably tiger sharks – and, in some parts of the world, they move into coastal waters to feed on turtles congregating near their egg-laying sites. Just swimming in a known sea turtle area could be enough to invite an attack.

When in the company of sharks: breathe deeply and slowly and avoid rapid or exaggerated movements; keep at least 5 m (16 feet), but preferably 10 m (33 feet), from the sharks; do not descend towards them from above; do not make them feel cornered or trapped; do not swim towards them at an angle of less than 45 degrees; avoid using your hands to maintain buoyancy; and do not attempt to chase, touch or ride them.

If a shark begins to show too much interest, or appears to be unhappy, the best response is to stay together – in fact, get as close together as possible – because, as a group, you demonstrate size, strength and confidence. Try to keep the shark in view and move away slowly. Get out of the water, if possible, but at least find somewhere with a bit of cover (such as on a reef), or move out of the area the shark appears to be defending. Professional shark-divers always ensure that they have a rapid means of exit, into a boat or on to dry land, and never get embarrassed about leaving the water if they sense an uncomfortable situation developing. If the shark persists, it may be possible (as a last resort) to push it

away with a gloved hand, camera or stick. Some experts recommend a hard hit on the snout to deter it from approaching too closely, but, unless the shark is actually attacking, others consider this to be provocative and it may produce an immediate aggressive response. Other experts prefer to avoid an attack by being the aggressor and swimming hard and fast towards the

Above: Anyone tempted to swim with these playful Cape fur seals in South Africa should be aware that they are a favourite prey of great white sharks.

shark, but, again, in some cases, this could actually provoke an attack. The statistics show that poking or striking at a shark, or swimming towards it aggressively, can have the desired effect, but also that it does occasionally provoke the shark even more.

Shark repellents and protection

The first full-scale study into potential shark repellents was commissioned by the US Navy during the Second World War as they and the Royal Navy wanted to reassure servicemen and their relatives concerned about downed planes and shipwrecks in 'shark-infested waters'. Unfortunately, they had little success in their endeavours, and the search for an effecive repellent continues unabated to this day.

Many potential shark repellents have been tested over the years: poisons and irritants, nasty waterborne scents, sea-marker dyes, sounds of various pitches, human sweat, and many other weird and wonderful substances, with dubious effect. Scientists have also tested some interesting theories, such as enveloping divers in inflated black plastic bags to disguise their shape and prevent body fluids leaking into the sea, and dressing a diver in black and white to imitate a sea snake (an idea that was

dropped when it was realized that some sharks eat sea snakes).

Most experts are cynical about the promise of any of these repellents and deterrents; the best help most of them can provide is moral support and a false sense of security. This was certainly the case when the US Navy bottled copper acetate – the only chemical that seemed to have any effect – and issued it to all military personnel at sea under the name 'Shark Chaser'. It may have boosted morale, but it was probably useless and, indeed, recent tests have shown that it may even have attracted sharks. Poles with explosive heads, and a hypodermic gas device called a 'shark dart' have also been used to kill or seriously injure sharks that threaten divers, but these are cruel and unnecessary, except in extraordinary circumstances. As with other deterrents, they encourage a false sense of security, which is more likely to result in an aggressive encounter, and they enable panicked divers to kill mostly harmless sharks.

Scientists quickly realized that, in order to find an effective shark deterrent, they needed to understand sharks better. So in 1954 they organized the first scientific meeting devoted to sharks to discuss their work and to identify the gaps in their knowledge. Nowadays we understand sharks a little better, but we have made surprisingly little progress in our search for a shark repellent.

Recent developments

Perhaps the most significant progress has been made in South Africa, where researchers have taken a rather different approach. They have ignored the role of smell in shark predation, focusing instead on the role of minute electrical fields – and the result is the battery-powered Shark Protective Oceanic Device, or Shark POD. It effectively encloses a human diver within a weak electrical field, with a range of 4–5 m (13–16 feet), which interferes with a shark's natural electrical receptors, known as the ampullae of Lorenzini. This disruption is believed to be irritating to the shark and may force it to move away. Humans, and most other forms of marine life without sensitive electroreceptors, are not affected by the electric field.

The main component of the POD is strapped to the diving cylinder, and this is linked by wire to a small plate attached to the diver's fin; there is a switch to turn it on before entering the water, and a warning light reveals that the unit is working. A few experts are still cautious about the POD's effectiveness, but it has been rigorously tested over a period of five years by Australian underwater photographers and shark experts Ron and Valerie Taylor, and by the South African Natal Sharks Board. They have found that the electrical field is sufficient to keep sharks a safe distance away, and even when 4.6-m (15-feet) great whites hit the edge of the field, they reacted immediately and retreated. After two weeks of testing the POD while free-diving with great whites off the coast of South Africa, Valerie Taylor commented that they 'felt invincible...there were a dozen or more sharks around...and they all kept their distance'. The Taylors had similar success with many other species, including bull sharks and tiger sharks. The only time the POD failed to work was during experiments when it

Opposite: With sufficient care and experience, it is possible to dive relatively safely with potentially dangerous pelagic sharks, such as this oceanic whitetip off the coast of Hawaii.

was switched off temporarily to allow the sharks to feed: switching it back on again did not encourage them to release their meal.

Variations of the POD are being developed for shark-proof surfboards, bodyboards, sailboards, canoes and life jackets. Its potential for commercial divers and even surfers (to avoid the need for destructive shark nets around surf beaches) is widely recognized. However, there is some concern about the risk of long-term impact on the sharks and it has already been banned at several shark-dive sites (including Aliwal Shoal, South Africa).

Stainless-steel and aluminium cages were originally developed in the 1960s to allow photographers to work safely around great white sharks. These days they are employed by photographers, researchers and tour operators to observe a number of large shark species in safety. In Australia, abalone divers have developed transportable shark cages to protect them while they are on the move.

Some professional shark divers wear protective steel-mesh suits and gloves. Developed in the early 1980s, these fit over a wetsuit and prevent a shark's teeth from penetrating the skin. An average-sized, single-mesh suit weighs about 9 kg (20 lb) and contains around 400,000 electronically welded rings, but there are several variations on this basic design: double mesh for the tremendous tearing power of tiger sharks; heavier steel made into smaller rings for makos and other narrow-toothed sharks; and even specially constructed metallic plates to distribute the pressure of bites by larger sharks. Chain-mail suits are highly effective and allow divers to swim freely among small- to medium-sized sharks (a large shark can crush an arm or leg in its mouth or even pull it right out of its socket), but are expensive. Nevertheless, they have become standard equipment for divers filming sharks in feeding situations, those who feed sharks for shark-watchers, and shark scientists.

Finally, coastal authorities have experimented with a range of barriers to keep dangerous sharks away from bathing beaches.

The latest designs are certainly effective, and there are claims of them reducing the incidence of shark attack by as much as 90 per cent. But they work by removing sharks in the immediate vicinity of the beaches, and not only do they capture the potentially dangerous species, they also capture sharks that pose little threat to people. A huge variety of other marine life, from dolphins to sea turtles, is caught and drowned in the nets, too. In KwaZulu-Natal, South Africa, shark nets were introduced in 1952 and they catch an average of 1245 sharks each year – mainly great white sharks, tiger sharks and bull sharks. Constantly looking at ways of reducing the environmental impact of the nets, the Natal Sharks Board has cut their total length from a peak of 44 km (27 miles) in the early 1990s to 29 km (18 miles) today – without jeopardizing the safety of bathers – and regularly checks them to release live animals. But they still work by killing sharks rather than deterring them. Similar nets are used in Australia: off the coast of New South Wales they are lifted during winter, when the water is cold and there are relatively few bathers, but in other parts of the country they remain in place all year round.

An 'inevitable' attack

When a diver was attacked by sharks on 23 July 1996, many experts concluded that the attack had been virtually inevitable. As Jeremy Stafford-Deitsch observes in his excellent book *Red Sea Sharks*, 'the attack culminated after several high-risk details came together'. It serves as an important warning to others.

The attack took place about 1 km (½ mile) off Marsa Bareika, Sharm El Sheikh, in the Red Sea. It was late in the afternoon when the diver and two friends went swimming in deep water with a small pod of five bottlenose dolphins. Soon after his friends had clambered back into the boat, leaving him alone in the water, the diver was attacked by at least two sharks. Experts concluded that they were probably tiger sharks. The largest bite was 46 cm (18

inches) in diameter, suggesting that one of the attackers was at least 4 m (13 feet) long. Three of the dolphins surrounded the diver and may have saved his life by beating their flukes and fins on the surface of the water to keep the sharks at bay until he could be rescued. He received four major bites but, thanks to the prompt application of tourniquets on the boat, emergency treatment in Sharm El Sheikh and rapid evacuation to the Egyptian military hospital at El Tur, he survived.

With the wisdom of hindsight, this diver was probably courting disaster. He entered the water late in the afternoon, which is precisely when many sharks are hunting, and in deep water, where larger and more dangerous sharks are more common. He swam with a group of dolphins, which are often accompanied by sharks seeking the same food or intent on hunting them. By splashing about on the surface, he would have given off vibrations that any sharks nearby would have mistaken for an injured animal, and the dolphins would have added to the cacophony by swimming excitedly around him. Without a mask, he would not have seen sharks in the area or been aware of any exploratory passes in time to get out of the water. Finally, he stayed in the water after his friends had returned to the boat, making a solitary target that sharks typically prefer. It really does appear to have been an accident waiting to happen.

What is particularly interesting about this attack is that a tiger shark at least 4 m (13 feet) in length could easily have bitten right through the diver; so although the resulting wounds were terrible and life-threatening, there is every chance that the shark was merely taking tentative, exploratory nips.

The bottom line is this: sharks possess such acute senses, are such powerful predators and have such a wide distribution that few people would emerge from the sea unharmed if they were really out to get us.

Opposite: It is a myth that if dolphins are in the water, there are unlikely to be sharks too.

Are sharks in danger of extinction?

Do commercial fisheries pose a real threat to sharks?

How serious is habitat degradation?

What is shark finning?

Is demand for shark products real or manufactured?

What can medical researchers learn from sharks?

How many sharks are killed as bycatch?

Which are the most endangered species?

What conservation measures are being taken?

Are sharks worth saving?

Sharks in Trouble
Under Threat Around the World

Sharks are in serious trouble. The threat they pose to us, in the form of shark attacks, is minuscule compared with the threat we pose to them. According to the most widely accepted scientific estimate, more than 100 million sharks are killed by people every year. However, many experts believe that the true figure could be closer to 150 million. No shark species has yet been declared extinct, although several are critically endangered and it is very likely that some have disappeared without our knowledge. A number of regional stocks have definitely gone – commercially and, perhaps, biologically extinct.

Sharks face many threats but two in particular account for the majority of deaths:

• Incidental capture by fisheries targeting other species. Drift nets, purse-seine nets and longlines set for other fishes catch many millions of sharks every year (along with a wide variety of other wildlife, from whales and dolphins to turtles and seabirds). Some estimates suggest that as many as 6.5 million blue sharks alone are taken as so-called bycatch every year.

• Commercial fisheries targeting sharks for their fins, meat, liver oil, skin, cartilage, gill rakers, teeth and jaws. Demand for these products has varied over the years, partly because of technological and cultural changes, but these days the greatest threat by far is the escalating trade in shark fins to make shark-fin soup. Demand for this expensive delicacy is now at an all-time high.

Sharks are also targeted by sports fishermen willing to pay considerable sums of money to catch fierce-looking 'trophy' sharks and, in some parts of the world, there is still considerable demand for shark jaws and teeth as ornaments and jewellery. Worried by declining catches, some sports fishermen have called for protective measures, but recreational fishing can still contribute significantly to shark mortality. In some areas there is a catch-and-release policy for the larger species, although even this is not without problems: the sharks are often released with hooks in the gut, throat or mouth, and these can cause serious injury or death.

Sharks are also killed deliberately by commercial fishermen determined to eliminate competition for 'their' stocks or to protect their nets. And several thousand die every year in the nets set around certain South African and Australian bathing beaches. Designed to protect bathers, these nets do not form complete barriers to keep sharks out, but merely reduce the number of sharks in the area by killing them (along with a lot of other marine animals).

Like most other wildlife around the world, sharks suffer from habitat degradation – as a result of coastal development and pollution. Habitat requirements vary from species to species and during different stages of their life cycles, but critical shark habitats include shallow estuaries, coastal bays, coral reefs, kelp forests, mangrove swamps and the open ocean. Many sharks – even some open-ocean species – use inshore pupping and nursery grounds. The juveniles may remain in these shallow waters all year round, taking advantage of the abundant food and shelter from predators, and without these safe nursing grounds many shark populations would be doomed. In the Mediterranean, for example, nursery areas close to shore are known to be used by a variety of local shark species, including the smooth hammerhead, the dusky and the great white. A very large human population lives within 100 km (60 miles) of the ocean, and an increasing amount of coastline is being developed for an ever-expanding tourist industry. The results are frightening: more than half the salt-marshes and mangrove swamps in the USA were lost by the mid-1970s, for instance, and a similar story of destruction is being repeated all over the world.

Another fear is that our demand for fish is insatiable – and this spells trouble for sharks too. We sweep the oceans clean with the help of fish-finding sonar and other modern technology, spotter helicopters, factory ships operating 24 hours a day, and enormous nets and fishing lines. Global fish consumption has almost doubled in less than 50 years, and to keep up with demand catches will have to double again in the next 25 years. As *Jaws* author Peter Benchley says, there are 'too many people with too much sophisticated fishing gear chasing too few fish'. So even if we did not catch a single shark, they would be in trouble because we are taking all their food.

Page 112: This smooth hammerhead drowned in a net designed to protect swimmers on a bathing beach in South Africa.
Opposite: Many sharks use shallow coastal waters as pupping and nursery areas, and yet these critical habitats are disappearing frighteningly fast.

Shark finning

The finning trade is by far the greatest threat facing the world's sharks. While shark meat, skin, liver oil, cartilage and other products have an inherent value, it is shark fins that drive the market. In a shop in Hong Kong, for example, shark fins may fetch as much as US$725 per kg (US$330 per lb), while shark meat yields no more than a few dollars per kilo.

Shark fins are so much more valuable than the rest of the shark that, as soon as they have been removed, the entire animal is normally thrown overboard to save storage space on the boat

for more valuable fishes. Until the recent demand for shark fin, the sharks in a catch were seen as 'trash' fishes and were often thrown back alive and intact. Now they die because they have become a profitable sideline. The fins comprise only a tiny proportion of a shark's body weight, so finning wastes 95–98 per cent of each animal. It is also incredibly cruel: the fins are frequently removed from the sharks while they are still alive. Dumped overboard with terrible injuries, the animals are left to die slow, agonizing deaths.

Demand substantially exceeds supply, and this, combined with such a high value, means that pressure on sharks for their

fins has now spread to virtually every corner of the shark-inhabited world. As fishermen everywhere have been alerted to the commercial value of shark fins, an industry that was previously limited to parts of Asia and to certain species is now global in nature and involves virtually every known species of shark. Fishermen are being approached by traders and offered good prices for fins, so, not surprisingly, inshore shark populations are being targeted and fished out for rapid, but short-lived, profits. And all this to make soup.

Preparing shark-fin soup is a complex process, involving many different stages. First the fins are blanched in very hot water, ready for the denticles to be scraped off; then they are placed in freezing cold water, which makes it easier to remove the supporting cartilage; after that, they are sun-dried on special racks, before being transferred to a cool drying-room to prevent softening; then they are refrigerated until the chef is ready. When it is time to cook them, they are soaked again (this time to remove the inevitable urinary odour), and finally they are made into soup using the chef's own recipe. The fibres take on a consistency similar to noodles, but have little flavour or nutritional value, so these days chicken or vegetable stock is added to improve the taste. The end result is a clear, glutinous broth.

Shark-fin soup is a traditional Chinese dish dating back thousands of years, reputedly to the second century BC. Once a rare delicacy consumed only by the Chinese aristocracy, it played an important role as an indicator of social standing: the status of Chinese families is said to have depended on their chefs' ability to prepare it. The soup was even an essential part of formal banquets during the Ming Dynasty (1368–1644).

Demand for shark-fin soup has spread throughout Chinese communities in Asia and the rest of the world relatively recently, increasing dramatically since the mid-1980s. There is now an insatiable market for shark fins of almost any size or type, and because of its traditional association with privilege and social rank the soup is almost an essential ingredient at important events, such as weddings, birthdays and during Chinese New Year celebrations. This is partly a result of the explosive growth of the Chinese economy and the rapid expansion of trade with the outside world during the last two decades of the twentieth century. More and more people in Hong Kong, Singapore, Taiwan and other Asian countries can now afford luxury food items. In mainland China alone, the growing middle class is currently estimated at 250 million, and they are all potential consumers

Opposite: Shark fins drying outside a fish market in Trincomalee, Sri Lanka.
Above: Juvenile scalloped hammerheads brought ashore by fishermen in Baja California, Mexico.

of shark-fin soup. There has also been a huge increase in oriental restaurants worldwide, adding to the demand. In addition, traditional Chinese medicine considers the soup to be an aphrodisiac and a tonic; it is supposed to strengthen the waist, provide a source of energy, nourish the blood, invigorate the kidneys and lungs, and improve digestion.

Ironically, far from being good for the health, shark-fin soup could actually be harmful. The way it is prepared – by drying out the fins – concentrates marine pollutants, such as mercury. Tests on shark fins conducted at the University of Hong Kong found levels of mercury were 5.84 parts per million (ppm), compared to a maximum permitted level of 0.5 ppm. Similar studies in the USA have revealed mercury levels up to 15 ppm – even before the fins were dried – and high levels of other heavy metals. The Hong Kong researchers also revealed that, because of the high mercury content, eating shark-fin soup could render men sterile – particularly ironic considering the number of people who consume it specifically for its supposed aphrodisiac properties. The sea is so polluted, and there are so many pollutants in sharks, that their fins really could be dangerous to eat.

Nevertheless, shark-fin soup sells for a high price in Asia. In Hong Kong, which is the biggest market and controls roughly

50 per cent of the global trade in shark fins, a single bowl of soup now costs as much as US$100 or more in specialist restaurants. The longer and thicker the strands, the better and costlier they are.

Some unscrupulous restaurateurs have been taking advantage of the fact that shark fin is tasteless, and there are reports of them putting fewer and fewer shark fins into their soup, sometimes even adding artificial fibres to make up the difference. Unfortunately, this has spawned an entirely new dish, consisting of whole, unbroken shark fin, which is popular with consumers determined to ensure that they are buying the real thing.

The fin trade, meanwhile, continues unabated. Data are incomplete because many countries do not report fin imports or exports, but from the relatively few figures available, it involves more than 125 countries around the world. Like the international trade in other wildlife products, it is nasty and ruthless, and the traders are not the kind of people easily persuaded by conservation arguments. There are claims that many of them have already made huge profits smuggling rhino horn, elephant ivory, bear gall-bladders, tiger bone and turtle shells. They have simply added shark fins to their inventory, or switched all their efforts to the shark-fin trade. There are huge profits to be made (shark fins are among the most expensive fish products in the world) and shark fins do not even have to be smuggled. No one seems to be as interested in the fate of sharks as they are in rhinos, elephants, bears, tigers and turtles, so the traders probably cannot believe their luck.

Other shark products

Sharks have been hunted for a variety of products since time immemorial, and at one time or another every part has been used for some purpose. The teeth of Greenland sharks were used by Inuit people to make knives; European artisans used shark skin to cover books, jewellery boxes and spectacle cases; Tasmanians

chopped up whole shark bodies to fertilize their orchards; and sponge fishermen in Florida threw the liver oil on to the surface of the water to help them see the bottom of the seabed more clearly.

Dried but untanned shark skin is called shagreen. Before the invention of sandpaper, it was used by carpenters to smooth and polish wood. It was also used to cover sword handles to provide a grip that would not become slippery when soaked in blood. After the denticles have been removed, shark skin can be turned into high-quality leather with several times the tensile strength of pigskin or cowhide; Texas and Arizona are major markets for shark leather, where it is used for cowboy boots, handbags and wallets.

Traditionally, shark meat is considered inferior, even unpalatable, food by many people, especially in the Western world. It can also be difficult to process because, if it is not bled, rinsed and processed quickly, the high urea content in the muscles gives it a strong taste and smell of ammonia. However, it is a popular dish in Asia, where many different shark species are eaten, usually dried, salted or smoked. The Japanese pay as much for shortfin mako meat, which is considered highly palatable, as they do for swordfish meat. More importantly, in India, Sri Lanka, Mexico, parts of Africa and other regions of the developing world, shark meat is a significant part of the diet, providing much of the protein requirements in poorer communities. In fact, as over-fishing depletes stocks of other fish, their reliance on shark meat is likely to increase in years to come.

The popularity of shark meat has grown significantly in the West in recent years because it is low in saturated fats and high in polyunsaturates, and therefore a healthier replacement for

Opposite, top and centre: Shark fins for sale in an Asian market.

Opposite, bottom: Greenland shark carcasses.

traditional red meat. The advent of shark hysteria may have helped to make it a trendy menu item in some countries, and recently the meat from shortfin mako and common thresher has begun to increase in popularity. French chefs particularly love the white, flaky, boneless meat of porbeagle sharks. There have been many marketing campaigns to overcome consumer resistance and shark meat is even sold under different names to diguise its true identity. The spiny dogfish, for instance, is sold in the USA as grayfish, in Britain as rock salmon, in France as *saumonette* ('little salmon'), and in Germany as *seeaal* ('sea eel').

During the nineteenth and early twentieth centuries, the huge, oil-filled livers of sharks sustained a large and important industry. The oil content of the liver varies from zero to more than 90 per cent, depending on the species and the maturity of the shark: a single basking shark can yield up to 500 kg (1100 lb). The oil is rich in vitamin A, and during the 1930s and 1940s many children gagged for their own good when they were forced to eat shark-oil extract. But the market collapsed in the 1950s, when Dutch chemists introduced a high-potency synthetic vitamin A, which could be manufactured on demand in great quantity and at a fraction of the cost of the original shark-derived product.

Shark oil also contains a colourless hydrocarbon, called squalene, which has been likened to ambergris (the waxy substance regurgitated by sperm whales and once used as a fixative in the perfume industry). Squalene was originally used to light lanterns, but continues to have many commercial applications, from lubricating fine machinery, such as watches and clocks, to being used for pharmaceutical products and as a skin rejuvenator in the cosmetics industry. Petroleum-based products have driven most of their shark-oil competitors from the market, but some cosmetics manufacturers still prefer squalene because it is the nearest inexpensive oil to natural skin oils.

Sharks have attracted a great deal of attention in medical research because they seem to be particularly healthy animals

and rarely get sick. Some of the attention is justified, some perhaps not. Shark corneas have been transplanted into humans, and the cartilage is a primary source of the compound chondroitin sulphate, a viscoelastic material used as a buffer in corneal transplants and cataract operations. Shark cartilage can also be used to make artificial skin for burn victims. In addition, it is sold as a dietary supplement in healthfood shops, and has been widely promoted as a miracle cure for cancer. But scientists conducting the research on which these products are based have publicly denounced their effectiveness, and a study published by the independent Cancer Treatment Research Foundation in 1998 concluded that shark cartilage did nothing to improve the quality of life or slow the disease in terminally ill cancer patients.

Fisheries bycatch

Some estimates suggest that at least half of all the sharks killed around the world are taken 'accidentally' by fisheries targeting other species. According to studies by the United Nations Food and Agriculture Organization, there are few fisheries that do not catch sharks as bycatch – and some are catching more sharks than the actual fish they are targeting.

Unfortunately, few precise figures are available. A huge number of sharks caught incidentally in fishing gear are simply thrown overboard and never appear in the official records. Even in countries where shark bycatch has to be reported, it tends to be *under*-reported. Another problem is that sharks are often categorized together because the fins from most species bear no distinctive markings, so regulators cannot determine the species of sharks or where they were culled. Hope for the future lies in using genetic identification techniques, but in the meantime it is possible only to monitor general trends in most parts of the world.

The number and species of sharks caught depends largely on the kind of fishing gear being used. Gear towed behind the vessel is particularly damaging. Bottom-trawl fisheries catch huge numbers of sharks in coastal areas, for example, while purse-seine nets used to catch tuna in the open ocean can also result in a massive shark bycatch. Drift netting, probably the most indiscriminate method of fishing ever devised, is another big killer of sharks, along with a wide variety of other wildlife. But the worst offender is probably longline fishing. With lines up to 65 km (40 miles) long the sheer number of hooks means that huge quantities of sharks are caught every year.

Evidence suggests that before the finning craze (when bycatch fishes were usually thrown back alive) that at least some,

Above: Worldwide demand for fish is insatiable and spells trouble for sharks because we are taking all their food.
Opposite: A fisherman sorts through shark carcasses and fins on a dockside in Taiwan.

and in a few cases many, of these animals survived. One recent study of a longline fishery in Hawaii estimated that 86 per cent of blue sharks caught as bycatch were alive when they were landed on deck, and even allowing for some later mortality, a large proportion of them would have survived had they been released instead of finned. Nowadays, though, fishermen can make a healthy profit from shark fins, and they cut them off before throwing the injured and dying sharks overboard.

There are ways of reducing bycatch, and some fisheries are doing this successfully already. The western Pacific pole-and-line fishery for tuna limits bycatch to less than 1 per cent of the total catch, and harpoon fisheries for swordfish and giant tuna have reduced recorded bycatch to nil. But in most cases efforts to do this tend to meet with substantial resistance from fishermen, who

are more concerned about the potential loss of extra income from the fins.

Endangered sharks

The World Conservation Union established the Shark Specialist Group (SSG) in 1991 to promote the long-term conservation of sharks and their relatives, the effective management of their fisheries and habitats, and, where necessary, the recovery of their populations. In June 1999, the SSG produced a Red List (updated a year later) of shark species known to be threatened with extinction. No fewer than 71 of the 450-odd known shark species appear on the list. Many others may also be in trouble, but there is not enough data available to determine their conservation status. More research is urgently required to fill in the gaps.

Every shark is listed according to its conservation status: 'endangered' means they are facing a very high risk of extinction in the wild in the near future; and 'vulnerable' means they face a high risk of extinction in the medium-term future.

The Red List includes a frightening number of familiar species, including even the great white, which is listed as 'vulnerable'. The sand tiger shark is also considered vulnerable worldwide, but is given endangered status in the southwest Atlantic and off eastern Australia (where it is more commonly known as the grey nurse shark); this large coastal shark has one of the lowest reproductive rates known among sharks, giving birth to just one or two young every two years, so its ability to sustain fishing pressure is very low.

Five sharks are listed as endangered or critically endangered worldwide, meaning that experts fear they could disappear altogether in the near future (if they are not extinct already):

▼   Whitefin topeshark – a little-known species from the Philippines, living in tropical inshore waters that are heavily fished and environmentally degraded. Only two free-living specimens are known and there have been no records for at least 50 years.

▼   Smoothback angel shark – a bottom-dwelling shark found over the continental shelf in the western South Atlantic. This is a late-maturing species (70 per cent of these sharks caught in Brazilian bottom trawls are immature) that lives in an area where sharks are fished intensively.

▼   Borneo shark – a rare inshore species, known only from five confirmed specimens (four of which were found in Borneo). It has not been recorded since 1937, despite several comprehensive surveys of the shark catches brought in by fishermen in the region.

▼   Ganges shark – until recently, this species was known from just three museum specimens that were hauled out of the Ganges-

Opposite: A sad reminder of the impact of fisheries on sharks: this oceanic whitetip was caught on a longline set in Mexico.

Hoogly river system over a century ago. Then, in 1996, a 2.8-m (9-feet) female was caught, confirming that the species was not yet extinct. If it still survives today, it is probably confined to the turbid waters of rivers and estuaries.

▼   Speartooth shark – another extremely rare shark known only from a single specimen collected 'somewhere in the Indo-Pacific' (the exact location has long been a mystery), although a few jaws found in Papua New Guinea may also belong to the same species. Like the Ganges shark, it is probably confined to the turbid waters of rivers and estuaries.

A number of other species are considered vulnerable on a world scale, but endangered in certain localities. The basking shark, for instance, is listed as endangered in the northeast Atlantic and north Pacific. It suffered heavy hunting pressure as the target of coastal harpoon fisheries off Scotland, Ireland, Norway, Iceland, France, Spain, Canada, California, Ecuador, Peru, China and Japan. It has been taken opportunistically by whaling vessels, and is caught as bycatch during other fishing activities. Past experience has demonstrated that basking sharks are extremely vulnerable to overfishing, and experts fear that serious population declines are likely if they are targeted again in the future.

Many other species are considered lower risk but 'near threatened', which means that they are already close to being vulnerable, and any increase in their exploitation will push them further up the Red List. These include the blacktip shark, sandbar shark, oceanic whitetip, bull shark, shortfin mako, tiger shark, blue shark and many other familiar (and less familiar) species. One inclusion that will shock divers in many parts of the world is the grey reef shark, a widespread species that was once common in clear tropical waters along the coast and around oceanic atolls. But its restricted habitat choice, site fidelity, inshore distribution and slow reproduction rate, combined with increasing unmanaged fishing pressure, are all causes for concern, so it is also listed as one to watch closely.

Entire populations of sharks are disappearing fast. A recent study at Dalhousie University in Halifax, Nova Scotia, analysed more than 15 years of logbook data collected by the US National Marine Fisheries Service, one of the longest records of shark statistics available. The records covered longline fishing in the northwest Atlantic and included nine species of shark. The results are frightening. Over the past 8–15 years, eight of the nine species experienced population declines of 50 per cent or more. The scalloped hammerhead population was the hardest hit, declining by 89 per cent between 1986 and 2002. Great white sharks and thresher sharks came a close second – their populations are estimated to have declined by over 75 per cent in the past 15 years. Quite simply, shark populations in the northwest Atlantic are in danger of extinction. And now that shark-fishing boats can go to almost every corner of the globe, and few shark populations are too remote to be exploited by modern fishing fleets, the same story is being repeated around the world.

The consequences

We know so little about most shark populations that the consequences of this dreadful onslaught of threats are largely unknown. But what we do know is that shark populations have a habit of crashing very quickly when they are fished, and then take many years to recover – if they recover at all.

The reason is that 'sharks barely replace themselves', as Professor Samuel Gruber, former chairman of the World Conservation Union Shark Specialist Group, once commented. They reproduce very slowly: some species are not sexually mature until they are in their mid-teens, a few have one- or two-year gestation periods, and others produce as few as one or two pups per year. Like other apex predators, such as lions, tigers and bears, they are at the top of the food chain, so their lives are not designed for heavy predation. Sharks are naturally accustomed to conditions of low natural mortality and simply cannot adapt by producing larger numbers of young to replace the huge numbers

now being killed by fishermen. Consequently, sharks suffer from overfishing even more than most other fish populations.

The spiny dogfish is a good example: the female does not breed until she is at least 12 years old, and gestation is up to two years; in her 70-year lifespan she will produce a maximum of 20 live pups. Nature intended for shark populations to remain small, and this, ironically, may hasten their downfall. It can take decades after fishing has stopped for them to grow and produce a new generation.

Worse still, for much of their lives many shark species are segregated according to their age or sex, so heavy fishing can completely eradicate an entire generation, or all the females or males, frighteningly quickly. If fishermen target a group of

mature females, for instance, the effect on breeding in that particular population can be devastating.

The end result is this: rising catches of sharks are followed by rapid population declines, and – even if the stocks are protected – very slow recoveries.

Some biologists believe that shark populations are so fragile, so biologically vulnerable, that they should never be exploited at all. Yet governments frequently encourage fishermen to take sharks (usually when more traditional species have been overfished and are no longer commercially exploitable), and even offer loans, subsidies and other financial or logistical support to help them make the change. Sharks have become the 'salvation' fishery of the past two decades, and they are being overfished as quickly as the traditional resources. To make matters worse, while most economically important fisheries are now controlled by catch and size limits, closed seasons, gear restrictions and other management practices, only a handful of the 125 countries involved in shark fishing and international trade have even the most minimal control measures in place.

This near-total lack of awareness and management includes a failure to compile shark-catch records in most parts of the world. Few countries have any statistics at all – and even fewer have reliable statistics. Specific and consistent monitoring of the catch and trade in sharks is urgently needed to fill the gap.

The little information that does exist for shark fisheries demonstrates a strong 'boom and bust' tendency, which does not bode well. The porbeagle shark fishery in the northeast Atlantic, for example, peaked at 8060 tonnes (7931 tons) in 1964, but has failed to exceed 100 tonnes (98 tons) since the late 1970s. Similarly, the soupfin shark fishery in California expanded spectacularly in the late 1930s (with the discovery that liver oil is rich in vitamin A), and peaked at 4000 tonnes (3936 tons) in 1940; the fishery crashed in 1942 and was down to only 300 tonnes (295 tons) by 1944. The population had been almost fished out in a few years, and may never recover.

Another classic example is the rise and fall of basking shark fisheries in many parts of the world. It is difficult to generalize, but most basking shark fisheries have taken hundreds or, typically, about 1000 individuals every year for a few years, before collapsing. The fishery based on the tiny island of Achill, off County Mayo on Ireland's west coast, was typical of this approach. It was a thriving fishery in the late 1940s, reaching a peak in

Pages 124-5: Grey reef sharks at Bikini Atoll in the Marshall Islands, Micronesia.

Opposite: Like many sharks, the spiny dogfish breeds so slowly that it can take decades after fishing has stopped for a population to recover – if it recovers at all.

1952, when no fewer than 1808 basking sharks were landed. But the relentless hunt ultimately (and predictably) forced the fishery into rapid decline, and from 1956 the catch dropped significantly. By 1966, the total annual catch was only 46 sharks, and the fishery eventually closed in 1975. It has been estimated that the shark population declined by over 80 per cent in less than ten years. The animals had all but disappeared from the area and even today, more than a quarter of a century later, basking sharks are still scarce there.

Shark researchers at the University of Miami were shocked to observe this boom and bust effect first hand, when they were studying lemon sharks in Florida. Their research involved catching the sharks with nets, tagging them, and then releasing them back into the sea. They netted more than 150 sharks in 1986, then only 42 in 1988, and just 14 in 1989; by 1990, there were virtually no sharks left and the research programme had to be closed. The population had suffered a huge loss as a direct result of commercial fisheries.

Taking shark conservation seriously

Most conservation groups are not fighting for shark fishing to be made illegal. As sharks are such an important source of protein in some parts of the world, a total ban would be impractical. It is the huge value of shark fins that is the problem, so what is really needed is an international ban on finning.

There are signs that some governments, at least, are beginning to take shark conservation seriously. A major break-through came on 6 June 2000, when the US House of Representatives passed the Shark Finning Prohibition Act by a landslide vote of 390–1. Shark finning had already been banned since 1993 in the US Atlantic and the Gulf of Mexico, but sharks in the US Pacific remained unprotected. A major concern was the number of blue sharks being killed by Hawaiian longline fishermen

targeting tuna and swordfish, which climbed from 2289 in 1991 to 60,857 in 1998 – an astonishing 2500 per cent increase. The sharks were caught incidentally but were being killed for their fins. The Act, which was formally passed by the US Senate on 7 December 2000 and became law on 13 March 2002, now makes finning illegal in all US waters. It prohibits the landing or possession of shark fins without the carcasses, and, since whole shark carcasses would compete for freezer space with much more valuable tuna and swordfish, this should make finning uneconomical for the fishermen. Prior to the US ban, shark finning was already banned in the waters of South Africa, Oman and Brazil, and it has since been banned in several other countries.

In Europe a shark fishing ban was proposed by the European Commission in August 2002. The planned measures would have outlawed shark finning by all boats in European Union (EU) waters, as well as by EU-registered vessels abroad, unless they had a special permit issued by their national authority, and on condition that the whole of the shark was used. It would also have included a package of measures for enforcement and new ways of monitoring the fin trade. But on 27 March 2003 the European Parliament voted against such a ban. Instead, it decided to allow the removal of fins on board, provided that the fins and bodies are landed together and that the vessel's cargo of fins weighs no more than 6 per cent of the live weight of the sharks. Conservationists were appalled by the decision because it is tantamount to a licence to fin hundreds of thousands of sharks. Effectively, it means that two out of every three shark bodies could be thrown overboard, and the vessels would still be able to produce the 'correct' ratio of fins to bodies on the quayside. Six per cent seemed excessive – for the species commonly caught in EU fisheries, 2 per cent of live weight would have been more than generous. Had the fishermen been forced to bring every shark back to shore, it would have made finning

unprofitable. Fortunately, though, on 5 August 2003 the decision was reversed and the original proposal reinstated. Now it has to go to the EU fisheries ministers for final approval.

But with so many countries involved in the shark-fin trade, and so many sharks migrating across international borders or living in international waters, there is an urgent need for a global agreement to protect and manage them properly. With this in mind, an International Plan of Action for the Conservation and Management of Sharks has been developed by the Food and Agriculture Organization. Unfortunately, although it includes many strong conservation recommendations, participation in the plan is voluntary, and it is designed primarily to ensure the long-term sustainable use of sharks.

Efforts to curb the shark-fin trade are also being made in other quarters. In the past few years, consumer pressure has prompted several Asian airlines to announce that they will no longer serve shark-fin soup to their Business and First Class passengers.

Another step forward came in April 1991, when South Africa became the first country in the world to protect the great white shark. It is now against the law to hook one within 365 km (230 miles) of the coast. Since then, the great white has been singled out for individual attention elsewhere in the world, and this once-maligned shark has been afforded varying degrees of protection in Australia, Israel, Namibia, the Maldives, the USA and several other countries. On 24 September 1999, Malta became the first European country to ban the fishing of great whites. It is a small step on a world scale, but if the most feared shark in the world can be given official protection, there is hope for the future. It demonstrates something of a U-turn in attitude:

Opposite: The basking shark fishery on the tiny island of Achill, off the west coast of Ireland, was closed when sharks all but disappeared from the area. This photograph was taken in 1954.

hostility has been replaced with concern by a more enlightened and much better-informed public.

Other sharks are beginning to receive similar treatment. Indeed, during the past few years, critical laws have been passed to protect several different species. Basking sharks are now protected in the USA, the Mediterranean Sea and in the waters around Britain; whale sharks are protected in the Philippines, Western Australia, the Maldives, India, Honduras, along the Atlantic and Gulf coasts of the USA, and in most other range states; shortfin makos are protected in Canada; and sand tiger sharks are protected in the USA and Australia.

In 2002, parties to the Convention on International Trade in Endangered Species (CITES) made history by extending the first-ever international protection to shark species. Both the whale shark and the basking shark – the world's two largest fish species – were voted on to Appendix II of the Convention. This allows trade in fins and other body parts only under strict rules. The resolution for whale sharks was proposed by the Philippines, India and Madagascar, and, although it was bitterly opposed by Japan, Iceland and other countries (who fought against CITES protecting any fish species), it managed to achieve the necessary two-thirds majority by just two votes. The basking shark resolution was proposed by the UK, on behalf of EU member states, and managed to achieve the necessary majority by just three votes.

There is still a very long way to go. Introducing official protection is one thing, enforcing it quite another. As with whaling, past experience has shown that shark fishing can be incredibly difficult to control, and there are cases where shark populations have declined dramatically, even after they have gained legal protection. The next challenge is to ensure that the world's sharks really do receive all the protection they deserve – at sea, as well as on paper. They have been a low priority for too long, and more investment is urgently needed in research, monitoring and management if their future is to look any brighter.

Why conserve sharks?

But does it really matter if shark populations, or even shark species, are allowed to disappear? Of course it matters, and there are several compelling arguments for shark conservation.

Since sharks are such an integral component of marine ecosystems, their disappearance is likely to disrupt the whole ecology of the oceans (in ways we know, and also in ways we are still discovering). The marine environment has evolved over millions of years to maintain a dynamic equilibrium, and each component is important in the grand plan. Sharks control their prey populations in a beneficial way, by removing the old, weak, sick, injured and genetically defective, and by scavenging on the dead. If they disappear, we can only guess at the possible knock-on effects further down the food chain. What we do know is that if we remove sharks, the grand plan will almost certainly be disrupted and the system thrown out of balance. This could have untold effects not only on local marine communities, but also on commercial fisheries. There is some evidence from field research and computer modelling work that this has already happened in some parts of the world.

Shark conservation also matters from an economical point of view. In many parts of the world, sharks are now worth more alive than they are dead. Divers pay substantial sums of money to see many species of sharks, and shark diving has become a multimillion-dollar business. Sharks that specifically attract divers to a particular coral reef (or any other diving location) are worth much more to the local economy than the relatively small one-off payment a fisherman would receive for their fins. In the summer of 1994, for example, the world-famous sharks of Sha'ab Rumi reef in the Sudanese Red Sea were caught by Yemeni fishermen working their way up the Red Sea reefs. Instead of

Opposite: These days many shark fishermen tag and release the sharks they catch instead of killing them and bringing their lifeless bodies back to shore.

providing a substantial income for a whole community for life, they provided a few fishermen a small income for a day.

From a selfish point of view, sharks may be able to help us in many different scientific fields. Aeronautical engineers and naval architects are studying their near-perfect hydrodynamic bodies in an effort to improve the design of aeroplanes, boats and submarines. Medical researchers are keen to understand how sharks heal their wounds within 24 hours without treatment, and how they resist all attempts to introduce cancer tumours; they are also trying to discover how they are nearly impervious to infections and circulatory diseases. Some species may hold secrets that one day could be used to fight human illness, but we will never know if we eliminate them from our oceans. Other researchers are intrigued by aspects of sharks' lives that we do not

fully understand, such as their ability to detect blood in very high dilutions and to osmoregulate in both fresh water and sea water.

Last but not least, the loss of such spectacular creatures would make the world's oceans much poorer places. This is an unquantifiable argument, but an ocean without sharks is unthinkable: like the Serengeti without lions, or Vancouver Island without killer whales.

How you can help

One of the greatest challenges in shark conservation is reversing, or at least mollifying, the traditional 'man-eating shark' image. A single person attacked by a shark makes headline news all over the world, but the relentless slaughter of millions of sharks attracts little attention. Whereas whales and dolphins have oodles of public sympathy on their side, sharks are still seen as the bad guys, to be reviled and destroyed. This attitude not only hampers conservation efforts, but actively encourages anti-shark measures. It has even been argued that fishermen are doing the world a favour by killing sharks and thereby making the oceans safer.

For us to wipe them out – through greed, need, fear, sheer recklessness or simple ignorance – would be a tragedy. But time is not on our side, and the problems can be solved only by us. If you would like to support shark conservation measures around the world, here are some useful website addresses:

Wild Aid: **www.wildaid.org**
American Elasmobranch Society:
www.flmnh.ufl.edu/fish/organizations/aes/aes.htm
European Elasmobranch Association:
www.dholt.demon.co.uk/elasmo.htm
Fiona's Shark Links Galore:
www.postmodern.com/~fi/sharklinks/links.htm
The Shark Trust: **www.sharktrust.org**

What is known about sharks' day-to-day life?

What are the main gaps in our knowledge?

Can all species of shark be successfully tagged?

How does satellite tracking work?

Where do basking sharks go in winter?

Have any new species been discovered recently?

What has been learnt from the megamouth shark?

Could sharks help scientists to find a cure for cancer?

What other human illnesses can they help with?

Shark Research
More Questions Than Answers

We have sent people to the moon and back, and unmanned spacecraft have travelled to distant corners of the solar system, yet we are only just beginning to explore the underwater world on our own planet. The oceans and their inhabitants are shrouded in mystery. We probably know more about the surface of Mars than we do about many marine animals, and our knowledge of sharks in particular has progressed surprisingly little since the naturalist Aristotle first took an interest in them more than 2300 years ago in the waters around Ancient Greece.

Our knowledge is minimal, and there is still much to learn: like all good scientific research, most shark studies are throwing up more questions than they are able to answer. But with the help of innovative research techniques, exciting new discoveries are being made all the time.

Until recently, most studies were made on dead sharks brought ashore by fishermen or collected by scientists, and on captive sharks in marine laboratories, so we have a reasonable understanding of their anatomy and physiology. Ironically, the expansion of commercial shark fishing has provided a wealth of such data in recent years because fishermen have had a vested interest in keeping more accurate and detailed records of their catches in order to identify shark hotspots. This information has helped to piece together a picture (albeit a rather sketchy one) of shark distribution. It has demonstrated that some species return to particular waters on a seasonal basis, for instance, and that some shark populations are segregated according to their sex and age. By providing plenty of dead specimens for dissection, it has also enabled scientists to examine the stomach contents of thousands of sharks to identify their favourite foods.

But we know virtually nothing about the lives and habits of sharks on a day-to-day basis. The real challenge now is to answer questions about what they get up to when they are living wild and free. How far and how fast do they travel? How deep do they dive? Where do they go to feed? Where do they go to breed, and what do they do when they get there? Why do males and females of certain species remain apart for most of their lives? These and many other questions remain unanswered for most sharks around the world.

Studying sharks in the wild can be incredibly difficult - not so much because they have sharp teeth but because, from a human perspective, they live in a relatively hostile, inaccessible environment. Unlike whales and dolphins, which have to come to the surface to breathe, sharks remain out of sight beneath the ocean waves for most of their lives. Finding them, let alone observing and following them, can be extremely difficult.

With the advent of the scuba system in the 1940s, and then chain-mail suits in the early 1980s, a handful of dedicated shark scientists began to take a hands-on approach and enter the water to observe their subjects face to face. In recent years these and other scientists have benefited from sophisticated high-tech equipment, such as acoustic and satellite tags, which are extending the boundaries of shark research still further. The main constraint these days is not a lack of expertise or technical know-how, but a lack of money. Serious science eats up large amounts of money, and serious financial support is usually available only for research that is likely to produce a profit or some benefit for humankind. Research into sharks for their own sake, satisfying a mere quest for knowledge, is much more difficult to fund.

Tagging

One of the most intriguing and productive areas of study involves tagging. Rather like bird ringing, this is an invaluable and cost-effective way of learning more about shark movements, growth rates and activities over days, weeks, months, or even years. Researchers secure or hold the shark alongside their vessel; attach a tag on or near the dorsal fin, or inside its body cavity; collect relevant data such as length and gender, the presence of mating scars, and the surrounding water temperature; then release it as quickly and efficiently as possible. Sometimes blood and tissue samples are taken for genetic analysis. Long-term studies have shown no detrimental effects from tagging, and, after all, sharks do considerably more damage to each other when they are mating or feeding.

The most basic tags are surprisingly simple, consisting of a non-corrosive numbered disc or dart with a sequential number and contact information for the tagging agency. They are normally attached to the first dorsal fin or in the muscles on

either side of the body just beneath the fin. These tags are cheap and easy to use but are only useful if the animals are caught later on in their lives, so the more sharks tagged, the better the chance of some being recovered. This research would be difficult without the help and support of fishermen, so in order to tag as many sharks as possible, researchers around the world have enlisted their help. Many sports fishermen have now stopped catching and killing sharks in favour of catching, tagging and releasing them, while commercial fishermen frequently return tagged sharks caught in their nets to the researchers (sometimes claiming special rewards in the process).

The largest tagging agency is the Cooperative Shark Tagging Program, sponsored by the US National Marine Fisheries Service, which enlists the help of no fewer than 6500 recreational and commercial fishermen throughout the northwest Atlantic and

beyond. Two principal tag designs are used: fin tags, used mainly on small sharks, resemble the ear tags used to identify cattle, and are attached to the first dorsal fin; dart tags, used for larger sharks, can be easily and safely implanted in the muscle near the base of the first dorsal fin while the animals are still in the water; they are composed of a stainless steel dart head, a monofilament line, and a plexiglas capsule containing a vinyl plastic legend with return instructions printed in several languages. Since this tagging program began in 1962, more than 171,000 sharks of 52 different species have been tagged off the eastern seaboard of North

Above: Many shark scientists have a hands-on approach and enter the water to observe their subjects at close range.
Page 132: Biologists in the Bahamas tag and release a young tiger shark.

America, ranging from just one scoophead shark to an impressive 93,494 blue sharks. No fewer than 10,000 sharks of 33 species have been recovered, including 5808 blue sharks. Eighty-six per cent of these recaptured sharks belong to just seven species: blue, sandbar, tiger, shortfin mako, lemon, blacktip and dusky.

The Cooperative Shark Tagging Program has solved some of the mysteries surrounding sharks in the North Atlantic. For instance, we now know that blue sharks mate off the east coast of North America, but then migrate to their pupping grounds thousands of kilometres away off the coasts of southern Europe and Africa. There is no better argument for international cooperation in both shark research and conservation.

Such collaborative efforts between researchers and fishermen are ambitious and impressive but, unfortunately, they have an important limitation: the tagging reveals only the starting point and recapture point of the shark. It gives little information about the shark's movements over the period in between, which, in some cases, can be 20 years or more.

More sophisticated tagging techniques can provide a solution to this dilemma. Acoustic or sonic tags emit ultrasonic beeps that are beyond the hearing range of both sharks and humans but can be heard with a hydrophone (an underwater microphone), so researchers do not have to wait in the hope that the tagged shark will be caught again in months or years to come. Their main drawback is a very limited broadcast range – typically less than a few kilometres – so the tagged sharks usually have to be followed by boat. This is both time-consuming and expensive, and there are fears that the continual presence of humans may alter the behaviour of the sharks being tracked.

Opposite: University of Miami graduate students inject a tiger shark with tetracycline to mark growth rings in its vertebrae.
Above: A Caribbean reef shark investigates a diver (wisely wearing a protective glove) in the Bahamas.

An alternative is the satellite tag, which is expensive to purchase and run, but has a broadcast range over the entire planet. Satellite tags work by sending data to satellites orbiting the Earth, which are then beamed back down to powerful receiving stations on the ground. Their main drawback is that they cannot send data from under water – they need to be at the surface for the information to be collected by the satellite.

A relatively new technique, called archival tagging, provides a possible solution. Instead of transmitting their data in real time, these tags simply store the information until they are recovered. Researchers program archival tags to detach and float to the surface at a specified time (they have been dubbed pop-up tags for this reason). They broadcast a signal as soon as they pop up, and this enables the researchers to locate and collect them. Pop-ups have several advantages over simple sonic and satellite tags: they are smaller and less obtrusive, because they do not have to transmit data continuously; they last longer; they provide information even if the sharks never rise to the surface; and, most of all, they do not need to be tracked by boat.

Archival tagging is being developed even further, with the help of stationary monitors on the sea floor. These monitors effectively turn areas frequented by shark populations into underwater sound studios: they record the time and date every individually identified, archival-tagged shark swims nearby. In the future, video cameras may be incorporated into the system: they will start filming as soon as one of the monitors detects a shark to provide researchers with an intimate glimpse into the private life of the animals under entirely natural conditions.

Both acoustic and satellite tags can transmit an incredible amount of information way beyond the mere location of the sharks, including their depth and compass bearings, the temperature of their muscle tissues and of the surrounding water, and even the pH (acidity or alkalinity) of their stomachs. With advanced electronic components and long-lasting batteries, many of these devices can transmit data for many months.

A variety of tags is being used by the Hawaii Institute of Marine Biology to study tiger sharks. The sharks are captured just off Honolulu Harbour, by setting lines baited with fish market scraps at dusk and recovering them at dawn the following day. Once secured alongside a small boat, they are measured and sexed, then a tissue sample is taken for genetic fingerprinting. Each shark is then fitted with a simple numbered identification tag. Individuals over 3 m (10 feet) are also fitted with a more sophisticated archival sonic tag. Researchers take advantage of the fact that, like many sharks, captured tiger sharks exhibit an extraordinary behaviour called 'tonic immobility' when they are

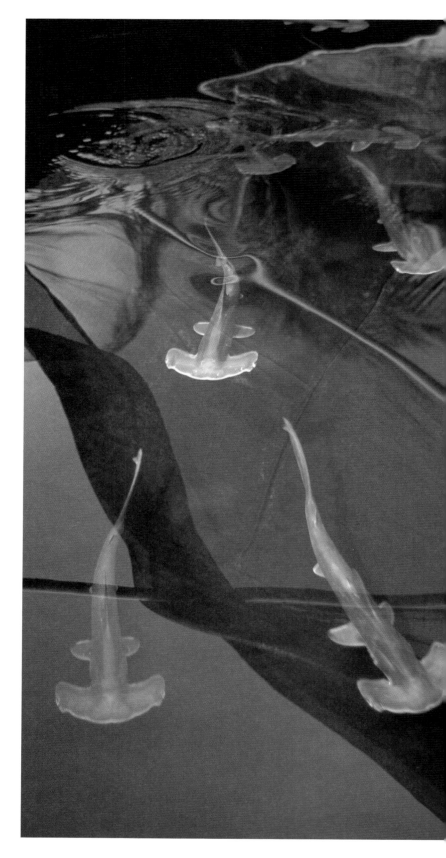

restrained and turned upside-down alongside the tagging vessel. If an active shark is turned over on its back, it goes into a kind of trance and can be handled with little fear of being bitten. It remains in its temporary coma for several minutes or more, then revives fairly quickly and swims away as if nothing has happened. Tiger sharks stay in this trance-like state for as long as 20 minutes, and this gives researchers plenty of time to insert the tag. The sonic tags used for this particular study are about the size of a beer can, and are surgically implanted into the peritoneal cavity (the space containing the liver and other organs).

The researchers are able to recognize individual sharks by their transmitter bleeps, and then track them by boat and with the help of special monitors placed by divers on the sea floor. The tags record information, such as depth and temperature, and this data is automatically downloaded every time the tagged shark passes by one of the monitors. So far, more than 130 tiger sharks have been tagged and released during the study, which is already gaining a valuable insight into tiger shark movements and home ranges. It has shown that tiger sharks seem to have very large home ranges – so far, they have all travelled more than 16 km (10 miles) during the first day of their release, and it has taken between two weeks and ten months for them to return to the original capture site. This is valuable information because it means that when a tiger shark is implicated in a shark attack, there is no point in trying to catch the individual responsible because it is likely to have disappeared elsewhere within hours of the incident.

One of the world's great wildlife mysteries is being investigated with the help of a tagging programme in the coastal

Opposite: Juvenile scalloped hammerheads in a research laboratory in Hawaii.
Above: Underwater researchers frequently put an extraordinary piece of shark behaviour called 'tonic immobility' to good use; if the shark is turned on to its back, it goes into a kind of trance.

waters of Britain, which is home to a significant population of basking sharks. The sharks are present during the spring and summer, from about April to September, and then disappear for the entire winter. With the notable exception of the central Californian coast (where, for some reason, they are more frequently encountered during winter), observations in other parts of the world suggest a similar pattern. Until quite recently, we had no idea where they came from or, for that matter, where they went. There was no evidence of a mass migration, and, in an effort to explain their annual disappearance, some experts even suggested that the sharks dropped down to the seabed to hibernate.

Following a giant fish some 10 m (33 feet) long might seem fairly straightforward, but it is by no means as simple as it sounds. Basking sharks can be tagged with very high-frequency radio tags, then tracked using a sophisticated TV aerial. Headphones in place, and standing on the bow or high in the crow's nest, the researcher listens for the tell-tale clicks that reveal the presence of a surface-feeding shark. 'Baskers' are among the few shark species that can readily be observed at the surface, so in reasonable weather, once they have been located with the help of radio tags, it is simply a matter of searching for their characteristic tall dorsal fins slicing through the water.

But as soon as the sharks disappear into the murky depths, they might as well vanish from the solar system. Tracking basking

sharks in their unseen underwater world – especially during the winter – was one of several challenges facing researchers who embarked on a three-year research project being funded by the Department for Environment, Food and Rural Affairs, the Centre for Environment, Fisheries and Aquaculture Science and the Marine Biological Association of the UK. To find out where the sharks go for the winter required the use of sophisticated Pop-up Archival Transmitting tags attached to the sharks' dorsal fins. Programmed to pop up to the surface at intervals of three, six, nine or 12 months, and then to beam their location and other information to an orbiting satellite many kilometres above the Earth, these tags have been fitted to basking sharks in the western English Channel off Plymouth and in Scottish waters off the Firth of Clyde.

Researchers successfully tagged ten sharks in the summer of 2001, and a further ten the following summer. Information has so far been recovered from six of the 2001 tags, and three of the 2002 tags. Two tags were recovered physically and provided minute-by-minute details of diving behaviour – one for no less than 8.5 months – while the others popped up on schedule and successfully sent summary data back via satellite. These recoveries alone are helping to solve that long-standing mystery – where do basking sharks go in the winter? – and results so far suggest that Britain's baskers remain on the European continental shelf throughout the winter. They do not appear to make long-distance migrations and do not, after all, hibernate on the seabed.

Above: A researcher using dye filament to study respiratory flow and smell in a nurse shark.
Opposite: The megamouth is one of the strangest and least known of all the world's sharks, discovered for the first time by accident in 1976.

Megamouth shark

Some of the more dramatic developments in shark research have involved the discovery of entirely new species. Sharks previously unknown to science are being found surprisingly regularly but a particularly large, black, blubbery shark, known as the megamouth, has been hailed as one of the most exciting wildlife discoveries of recent years.

This strange, plankton-feeding shark, with an exceptionally large mouth, great fleshy lips, protruding jaws and thousands of tiny hooked teeth, was discovered for the first time on 15 November 1976. Until then, there had never been any hint that it ever existed, and, not surprisingly, the find was described as the shark discovery of the century. The US Navy research vessel *AFB-14*, operating at a depth of 4600 m (15,000 feet) some 42 km (26 miles) northeast of Oahu, Hawaii, deployed two parachutes as sea anchors at a depth of about 165 m (540 feet). When the chutes were hauled to the surface, the crew spotted something caught up in the fabric. It proved to be a male shark some 4.46 m (14 feet 8 inches) in length and 750 kg (1650 lb) in weight. Shark experts examined the dead body, dubbed the creature 'megamouth', and gave it the scientific name *Megachasma pelagios* – 'yawning mouth of the open sea'. A new family, genus and species of vertebrate was specially created to classify this weird and wonderful monster of a shark.

A second dead individual was caught by commercial fishermen off Catalina Island, southern California, on 29 November 1984. Since then, about a dozen other dead specimens have been found (either caught by fishermen or washed up on shore) as far afield as Japan, the Philippines, Senegal, Brazil and Western Australia. A healthy, live megamouth was seen for the first time on 21 October 1990, when a fisherman caught one alive off Dana Point, southern California, and towed it into the harbour. On 23 October, after hordes of ichthyologists had studied it and camera crews had filmed it, the shark was released back into the Pacific with a radio tag attached.

The megamouth has a soft, uncalcified cartilage skeleton, a flabby body and relatively weak muscles thought to be sufficient only for slow, steady swimming. Its tail fin, which is asymmetrical with a greatly elongated upper lobe, also suggests that it does not swim particularly fast. Circular scars on its skin suggest that it is frequently attacked by cookie-cutter sharks. The radio-tagged individual (which scientists were able to track for two days) migrated up and down in the water column, rising to within 15 m (50 feet) of the surface at night, and dropping to depths of about 150 m (500 feet) during the day. Experts believe that it was following the daily migration of shrimps, pancake sea jellies, copepods and other prey animals, which it filters out of the water with its gill rakers. It has an enormous tongue, which almost fills its closed mouth, and this may be used to compress its catch against the roof of its mouth, a technique similar to that used by baleen whales.

We know very little else about the megamouth. The fact that it lives in the open ocean, often at great depth, may explain why it is so rarely encountered, and will certainly make it a challenging creature to study.

Above: A lemon shark with scientists in the Caribbean.
Opposite: Measuring the metabolism of a captive
juvenile hammerhead shark in Hawaii.

Sharks in science

An entirely different field of research focuses on the potential value of sharks to people. Scientists are particularly keen to find out how they have managed to survive for hundreds of millions of years in oceans teeming with bacteria and viruses, and, more recently, with cancer-inducing pollutants. Sharks do get sick, but surprisingly rarely. They do not appear to succumb to illness and disease as much as most other animals – certainly not as much as people – even though they are exposed to essentially the same hazards. If we could find out how they keep so healthy, it might be possible to improve our own health.

Cancer is a particular area of interest. Few wild sharks have been found with cancer and experiments exposing captive sharks to potent carcinogenic chemicals result in a very low incidence of cancerous tumours. Scientists are therefore keen to find out how sharks have developed a level of immunity to cancer. One theory is that shark DNA does not mutate easily (genetic mutations are implicated in many cancers caused by prolonged exposure to toxins or radiation), but there are several other possible explanations. Whatever the reason, there is hope that some day this research will find applications in boosting the human immune response to cancer. Shark liver, for instance, is a rich source of a steroid called squalamine, which could help to tackle potential tumour cells.

The immune system in sharks is actually quite primitive and not as well developed as it is in most mammals. In broad terms, it is comparable to the immune system in a human foetus, but while a human's immune system develops as it grows older, a shark's does not. It seems to be rather sluggish in its response, and will reject incompatible grafts, for instance, very slowly; by contrast, our own highly efficient immune systems reject them very quickly. Shark immune systems also seem to have no built-in memory for previous invasions of bacteria or viruses. They respond by producing antibodies, as our bodies do, but their response remains the same regardless of how many times the same

invaders have attacked while ours improves with each attack. But simplicity is not necessarily bad: low-tech systems are easier to fix than high-tech ones, and in the case of sharks it clearly works remarkably well.

Sharks are also being studied for a wide range of other medical purposes. The corneas from their eyes are already being used in some human transplant operations; artificial skin grown from shark-fin cartilage is being used in grafts to heal serious burns; the mechanism used by sharks to remove salt from their bloodstream has been adapted for the treatment of cystic fibrosis; shark blood is known to contain an anticoagulant (an anti-blood-clotting chemical) which may prove to be useful in treating patients with certain forms of heart disease; and shark gall bladders have even been used in the treatment of acne.

Scientists designing aeroplanes and boats are also taking an active interest in sharks. Tiny grooves on their dermal denticles, for instance, can significantly reduce drag: a reduction in drag of just 1 or 2 per cent could save the airline industry billions of dollars in fuel costs, and could help engineers to design safer planes.

Much of this work is still at an early stage. But there is little doubt that sharks hold the solutions to many perplexing problems facing scientists today, so there is huge potential in these avenues of shark research.

Shark Watching
Face-to-face Encounters

Many people never get over their fear of sharks. They would sooner leap off a cliff on to jagged rocks hundreds of metres below than jump off the back of a boat into a milling crowd of hungry sharks. Their fear is real enough, and, given the terrible reputation of these sophisticated predators and their formidable jaws and teeth, perhaps it is not surprising that the natural reaction is to do anything possible to avoid a face-to-face encounter. But shark watching is incredibly popular in many parts of the world, and a close encounter with a shark is considered by many to be the ultimate wildlife experience.

Being afraid of sharks is rather like being afraid of the dark – the imagined dangers are far worse than the reality. Those of us who do get close to them consider spending time with wild sharks to be a very special privilege. Every year, hundreds of thousands of divers around the world choose to jump into seas full of them. They pay good money to meet great whites, oceanic whitetips, shortfin makos, basking sharks and many other species – and live to tell the tale.

Shark watching is addictive. Observing such remarkable creatures in their own underwater world is awe-inspiring, and rubbing shoulders with such powerful hunters is thrilling. One close encounter is never enough, and the desire to see more is almost insatiable. See one shark and you simply have to see another...then another...and another.

The growth of shark diving

In the late 1960s and early 1970s, a few pioneering dive operators (particularly in the Maldives and the Bahamas) began to take recreational divers on organized shark encounters. This was quite a bold step, taken at a time when the general consensus was that anyone diving with sharks *intentionally* must be completely mad, reckless or outrageously adventurous. But the first shark watchers survived unscathed, and, slowly but surely, other dive operators began to follow suit.

This once-unlikely industry has been growing exponentially ever since, and shark watching is now big business. There are no precise figures on the scale of the industry, but commercial shark-watching trips are currently available in more than 40 different countries around the world and they have become an everyday occurrence. There have never been more opportunities for encountering sharks than there are today, and the sheer variety of trips on offer is astonishing. It quickly becomes a lifelong passion.

In California, off the coast of San Diego, divers descend 3–4 m (10–13 feet) to a cage suspended in the open ocean, with the seabed more than 1.6 km (1 mile) below, to watch blue and shortfin mako sharks. Cages are also used at the remote island of Guadalupe, off the Pacific coast of Mexico, for dramatic close encounters with large great whites.

In the warm waters of the Burias Strait in the Philippines, snorkellers participate in a research project studying harmless whale sharks, while in a shallow bay at Walker's Cay in the Bahamas even more adventurous snorkellers slip off the rocks to mingle with as many as 15 huge adult bull sharks.

Divers in Rangiroa Atoll in French Polynesia are swept along in a strong current in the company of grey reef sharks and whitetip reef sharks. And one of the most challenging shark dives takes place at Cocos Island, a long day-and-night sail off the coast of Costa Rica, where divers descend as low as 40 m (130 feet) to look up at hundreds of schooling scalloped hammerheads.

At the other extreme, in some parts of the world you can see wild sharks without even getting your feet wet. Walkers strolling along the elevated wooden boardwalks at Elkhorn Slough in California can observe leopard sharks and other species in the shallow waters underneath; and in Canada there have even been trips to observe sixgill sharks 200 m (660 feet) below the surface from inside a deep-sea submersible.

Attracting and feeding sharks

There seems to be a commonly held belief that there are so many sharks in the world's oceans, and they are so inquisitive and aggressive, that divers must come across them almost every time they dip a toe in the water. It is true that there are places, such as Protea Banks in South Africa and the Marshall Islands in Micronesia, where a normal dive is likely to result in a heart-stopping close encounter with a shark – whether you like it or not.

But elsewhere in the world, shark sightings are surprisingly few and far between. The sad fact is that there are not as many sharks as we are sometimes led to believe, and, at the same time, most of them are surprisingly shy. If a diver is fortunate enough to see one, it is often little more than a brief glimpse of a rapidly disappearing tail.

Above: A great white shark dwarfs divers in a cage off the coast of Dangerous Reef, Australia.
Page 144: A bait ball lowered into water attracts Caribbean reef and nurse sharks, which can then be observed at close range by divers.

Dive operators offering shark-watching trips need to be able to guarantee close encounters with the ocean's apex predators (as much as any wildlife encounters can ever be guaranteed), and in many cases the only way to do this is to use a type of bait, called 'chum', to attract the sharks artificially. Some operators use mammal blood for this, but chum normally consists of small fish, such as herring or mackerel, which are ground up into a liquid mash and then released gradually into the water to form a slick on the surface. Sometimes the chum is unceremoniously dumped overboard, but it may be kept in a perforated container

Huge numbers of sharks of several different species are attracted to a regular feeding site with the help of a large quantity of fish bait mixed with water. This is frozen around a metal bar, like a giant fishy ice lolly or 'popsicle' – hence its name 'chumsicle'. This is both anchored to the seabed and suspended from a float, ensuring that it hangs in mid-water. Divers are free to swim around it – along with the sharks.

Not all sharks can be coaxed in with bait, and not all shark dives involve chumming or feeding, but in many cases, without it, divers would not have the chance to see and photograph sharks close up. The lure of the bait is the guarantee of success. But using chum and, in particular, providing food for sharks is very controversial.

Is shark feeding acceptable?

Certain aspects of shark diving are controversial, and shark feeding in particular is a subject of heated debate among divers, tourists and conservationists. This is a complex issue and the potential risks and benefits of chumming and feeding are very different from country to country, location to location, species to species and even from season to season. Unfortunately, there are no simple answers: until we know more about sharks and the impact of different shark-chumming and feeding techniques, much of the debate will rely on conjecture.

The Cayman Islands took the matter seriously when, in January 2002, it passed a law (as part of a comprehensive Marine Conservation Legislation package) that prohibits feeding sharks under water or attracting them with chum tossed from boats. The law was passed with little fanfare, but it carries penalties that could include fines of up to $500,000, six months in jail and/or confiscation of the guilty party's vessel.

A major turning-point came in a blaze of publicity during the same month, when Florida became the first state in the US

under water or dripped into the sea via a hosepipe or through a hole in the hull.

It can take anything from a few minutes to several hours or even days for the chum to attract sharks. When they arrive, they swim around the boat expecting to find food, and if there is nothing more substantial than a slick of chum, they will leave to search for 'proper' food elsewhere. So the dive operators need to keep them interested with the help of bait – something the sharks can really get their teeth into. The bait may simply be hidden under a coral head, or placed in a sealed container, which is then opened by a pull-cord. Or it may literally be handed piece by piece to individual sharks by a professional feeder. One of the more innovative variations can be seen at Walker's Cay in the Bahamas.

Opposite: A chumsicle – a giant fishy popsicle or ice lolly – is used to attract sharks.
Right: Feeding sharks by hand, as shown here with a grey nurse shark in the South Pacific, requires a tremendous amount of skill and experience.

to prohibit divers from feeding sharks. Although the vast majority of shark dives do not involve chum or bait, the decision has provoked strong reactions from both the environmental movement and the diving industry. The Worldwide Fund for Nature, Defenders of Wildlife and others immediately hailed the ban as a major victory for wildlife and divers. The Florida-based non-profit Marine Safety Group said that 'divers all over the state will once again be able to enjoy the natural beauty of the undersea world without being continually mugged by aggressive fish seeking handouts'. But commercial dive groups, including the Professional Association of Diving Instructors, *Rodale's Scuba Diving* magazine and *Skin Diver* magazine, were very unhappy about the decision. A recent *Rodale's* editorial said that the ban 'provides a classic example of the triumph of fear over reason'.

Supporters of the Florida shark-feeding ban argue that shark feeds:

▼   dim the natural fear sharks have for humans (and vice versa);

▼   attract a larger number of potentially dangerous sharks into an area;

▼   encourage sharks to associate people with food;

▼   encourage sharks to grow dependent on 'free lunches' (which could ultimately change their distribution and hunting patterns).

They also argue that sharks should be viewed in their natural state and should not be trained to become 'circus sideshows'.

Critics of the ban argue that:

▼   there is no evidence that commercial shark-feeding has increased the risk of attacks on humans, pointing out that (at the time) the nearest confirmed attack to any shark-feeding operation in Florida was 160 km (100 miles) away;

▼   only a handful of Florida-based dive operators have been involved in shark-feeding;

▼   the two shark species being fed (nurse and Caribbean reef) have been implicated in just one of the recent attacks in Florida;

▼   fishing boats have been chucking huge quantities of fish offal overboard every day since time immemorial, with no measurable effect on the incidence of shark attack, so the relatively small amounts of bait being thrown into the sea during shark dives will have little or no impact.

Left: Divers meet sharks around a bait ball at Walker's Cay in the Bahamas.

Opposite, top: Dyer Island and Geysir Rock, South Africa – one of the best places in the world to observe great white sharks.

Opposite, bottom: A lone snorkeller enjoying a group of bull sharks in shallow water at Walker's Cay in the Bahamas.

They also claim that the decision was made in order to 'satisfy political and public pressure to respond to the hysteria generated by the media over a below-normal summer of shark bites in Florida and around the world'.

The shark-feeding ban in Florida is particularly noteworthy because the state has long been a hotspot for shark attacks. The year 2002 was fairly typical when, according to the International Shark Attack File, there were 60 confirmed cases of unprovoked shark attacks around the world, and 29 of them occurred in Florida. This was slightly lower than in previous years (72 unprovoked attacks were recorded in 2001, and 37 of them were in Florida) but the fact remains that Florida is *the* world hotspot for shark attacks.

Many possible reasons have been proposed, ranging from the sheer number of people in the sea to the fact that Florida is home to many potentially dangerous sharks. It must also be relevant that, in 2002, no fewer than 18 attacks (considerably more than half the total) happened in one place – on the central east coast, in Volusia County, where surfers gather at an inlet near New Smyrna Beach. Some 10–15 surfers are bitten here in an average year (there were no fewer than six attacks over a single weekend in August 2001), and the inlet has a reputation for having more shark attacks than anywhere else in the world.

Shark feeding is another reason proposed by advocates of the ban. There is some circumstantial evidence – but no conclusive evidence – of a direct link between the level of shark feeding and the incidence of shark attacks. On 16 March 2002, less than 200 m (650 feet) from a Florida dive site where dive operators had reputedly been feeding sharks illegally, a snorkeller was attacked by a nurse shark. And on 9 April 2002, the ISAF concluded that a diver was killed by a shark at the wreck of the *Ronald B. Johnson* – less than 2 km (1 mile) from a once-popular shark-feeding site.

Then, in June 2002, less than six months after the ban came into effect, a 16-year-old boy was attacked by a shark off St George's Island. He was bitten on the left foot while floating on a raft less than 25 m (80 feet) from shore, but close to an area where locals and tourists had been fishing and feeding gulls. The young lad made a full recovery, but the debate about whether there was a link between the attack and local fishing and feeding activities continues, and, inevitably, has added fuel to the shark-feeding controversy.

In the same month, Hawaii became the second US state to ban shark feeding. The ban became law (with virtually no opposition) on 6 June 2002, and forbids businesses from advertising or soliciting shark feeding. The Administrator of the Division of Aquatic Resources said that the new law takes a precautionary approach and 'prohibits such activities before they become established in Hawaii'.

The Marine Safety Group plans to take its fight to new battlegrounds in the future and is optimistic that other US states will soon follow suit with bans of their own. Commercial dive interests, meanwhile, have vowed to reverse the decisions. It is clear that passions over the issue have not abated.

Developing a responsible industry

There are four main considerations in developing a responsible and environmentally friendly shark-diving industry: the safety of the participants; the safety of swimmers, surfers and other water users nearby; the impact on the sharks; and the risk of ecological disruption.

The safety of the participants on a shark dive is paramount. It is essential for operators to put safety first, which means training divers in shark-friendly behaviour and warning them about the inherent risks. Then, in theory, it is up to the divers themselves to make an informed decision about whether or not to participate in the dive. Unfortunately, it is not that simple because some operators are far less responsible than others. The worst are both inexperienced and reckless, and may take extraordinary risks to make extra money or put on a show of bravado. There have already been a number of serious accidents: most recently, a woman on an organized shark dive in South Africa had to have 37 stitches in her hand after being bitten by a sand tiger shark. A serious accident could also undermine worldwide efforts to protect sharks by reinforcing the *Jaws* image. But to put this risk into perspective, even without proper regulation, the number of 'incidents' during shark dives is minuscule. There are no precise figures, but the order of magnitude is likely to be well within the acceptable limits of most popular adventure sports.

The safety of other water users near shark-dive sites, especially where the creatures are being attracted with chum and then fed, is far more controversial. The Bahamas is a good example. There are many potentially dangerous sharks in the waters around the archipelago, and many long-established shark feeds take place here every day, and yet there are surprisingly few shark attacks (just one in 2002). Nonetheless, even here, the finger of blame for shark attacks is often pointed at local dive operators – not least in August 2001, when a man lost his leg to a shark while swimming off a beach on Grand Bahama Island within 2 km (1 mile) of an established shark-feeding site. In South Africa, a recent spate of six attacks on surfers and divers within a five-week period prompted accusations that the cage-diving industry was responsible, but only one of these attacks occurred within 150 km (93 miles) of a cage-diving site; other environmental factors, such as the proximity of sardine schools, were more likely to blame.

These are exactly the kind of incidents that led to those shark-feeding bans in the Cayman Islands, Florida and Hawaii. One possible compromise is to create guidelines for shark feeding. These already exist in some parts of the world, and might include: a requirement to locate feeding sites away from living reefs and to use a zoning system to separate them from areas frequented by other water users; a limit to the number of feeding sites and the frequency of feeds; and compulsory diver education programmes.

Another concern is that all these human admirers will love the sharks to death. We have a responsibility to cause as little disturbance as possible: proper respect and etiquette are the most important tools of the trade. Yet, in some places, there is little doubt that the sharks have not been receiving the respect they deserve. Until remedial action was taken, one of the worst examples was in South Africa, where operators taking divers to see great white sharks around Dyer Island were literally fighting over limited anchorage space and using bait-filled nets to catch the sharks and haul them alongside their boats to give their clients a better view. The scramble by dive operators for a piece of the action (and the cowboy mentality of some) ultimately led the South African government to impose urgently needed regulations. Other governments have followed suit with similar efforts to control the new industry, going far beyond guidelines merely for shark feeding. These may be voluntary or legally binding, and include, for example, a limit on the number of boats licensed to operate shark dives and a minimum amount of equipment that must be carried on board (such as a working radio and trauma kit), as well as regulations concerning staff experience and qualifications, and the kind of bait and baiting techniques permitted to attract the sharks.

The risk of ecological disruption is perhaps the most difficult concern to quantify. Critics argue that the large concentrations of sharks at established feeding sites are unnatural and that the sharks may stop feeding on their natural prey if the alternative is an easy meal provided by dive operators. It has also been argued that these two concerns (too many predatory sharks *and* less predation) cancel one another out. In truth, the impact of shark feeding on the local ecology is largely unknown. Another ecological concern is easier to quantify and solve: while many operators use the fish remains discarded by commercial and sports fishermen for their bait, others actively hunt local fishes (even juvenile sharks in at least one dive site) and undoubtedly this could come to harm local populations.

Parallels with whale watching

Shark diving has some interesting parallels with whale watching. The whale-watch industry was growing exponentially before most people had even considered the possibility of diving with sharks. At first, it went largely unregulated. But to protect the whales, and the whale watchers, many countries introduced guidelines to bring the industry under control. As our experience and knowledge of whale watching continue to increase, these guidelines are being improved and adapted accordingly. Many whale experts would prefer not to have such a colossal whale-watching industry, but accept it as essential in order to achieve and maintain a high level of public support for whale conservation and research. We are still going through a similar process of enlightenment with sharks, and now that the shark-diving industry is showing a comparable exponential growth rate, it is beginning to face similar challenges. The challenge is to learn from the mistakes of the whale-watching industry and get it right sooner rather than later.

The value of shark diving

It is also important to remember that shark diving can directly benefit the sharks: it provides a much better alternative to hunting (making the sharks worth more alive than dead) and ensures that more people are better informed.

A dead shark is worth relatively little for its fins, but now that shark diving has become a multimillion-dollar business, a living shark can be worth a fortune. According to one study, a single reef

shark is worth US$100,000 every year to local businesses. Better still, it provides a source of income for life, not just for the short term, and benefits many different people. When divers visit an area to see the local sharks, they patronize hotels, guesthouses, restaurants, cafés, shops, buses, taxis and many other businesses, as well as the dive operators. This financial value also gives people a vested interest in protecting sharks. In the Bahamas, for example, when rogue fishermen wiped out the sharks associated with a feeding operation, there was such an outcry that the government banned longlining of sharks once and for all.

Above: Shark-diving has some interesting parallels with whale-watching, and those wanting to develop guidelines and regulations can learn a lot from the long-established whale-watching industry.

Shark diving can also help to dispel some of the myths about sharks and to change attitudes towards these much-maligned creatures. The sharks themselves make terrific ambassadors for marine conservation, lighting an internal fire that makes people determined to do something positive to help – but it is up to the dive operators to ensure that their captive audiences are well-informed. There is still a long way to go in this respect, and the opportunity to dive with sharks does not necessarily result in an improved understanding of and respect for them, but there are already a great many operations that show respect for sharks and provide accurate information about their natural history and conservation. They drum up public support for their cause by swelling the ranks of shark devotees, and ensure that part of the income from shark diving helps to fund urgently needed research

and conservation work. There is no doubt that sharks need as much help and support as they can possibly get and, in a unique way, professional, responsible shark diving has the potential to help enormously.

Ultimately, there are two fundamental challenges: to improve the overall quality of shark-diving tours and to do more research. When we understand how to arrange our meetings with sharks, we will be in a stronger position to ensure that there are more good operators than bad ones.

Above: Who is supposed to be watching whom?
An inquisitive Caribbean reef shark with equally inquisitive divers.
Opposite: A sand tiger shark cruises past the wreck of the *Caribsea* off the coast of North Carolina, USA.

Planning a shark dive

Provided you are already a qualified diver (or, in some circumstances, a confident snorkeller), the next step is careful planning, which is essential to ensure that your encounter is safe, environmentally friendly, successful and memorable.

While it is not essential to join an organized shark dive at a known hotspot, it certainly helps. It is safer to dive with sharks in the company of experts, and the probability of seeing a particular species is much higher.

First of all, decide what species you would most like to see. Many sharks are not only restricted to certain parts of the world, but may congregate there for only a few months of the year, so proper timing is crucial. One of the best places to see whale sharks, for example, is Ningaloo Reef in Western Australia, but

you have to go there from mid-April to the end of May to have a good chance of a close encounter.

Next, think about live-aboard dive boats versus shore-based diving. Sometimes, where the best diving is in a remote location, there will be no alternative: to see silvertips in Papua New Guinea, for example, you normally have to join a live-aboard dive boat for at least a week. But at many shark hotspots there is a choice between staying in a hotel on shore or joining a one- or two-week trip on a live-aboard dive boat. Staying on shore may suit non-diving partners and children better, enables you to include other activities in your holiday and makes a shorter, less expensive stay possible. It is also a good alternative if you just want to test the water with your first shark dive. In the Bahamas, for example, a half-day trip at any time of the year can virtually

guarantee sightings of Caribbean reef sharks. But live-aboards are probably better if your main aim is to pack in as much diving in as many different dive sites as possible.

The golden rule is to choose your dive operator with great care. The quality and performance of shark dives vary enormously, and your choice of operator can make or break the holiday. Be wary if one deal is much cheaper than another, and ask friends for recommendations, read dive magazines and check websites for further information.

If you plan to attend a shark feed, make sure that a few basic rules are enforced. The bait should be readily accessible to the sharks and should not be presented in such a way that it could harm them. Live fish should never be speared in front of the sharks because they might become agitated and, of course, spearfishing is illegal on many reefs. Divers should position themselves at least 3 m (10 feet) away from the bait and must not be down-current because sharks are likely to sample anything (including divers) inside the scent trail. Never, under any circumstances, try to hand-feed the sharks yourself: it is a skill that requires detailed knowledge and a steep learning curve, so should be left to the professionals.

There are many advantages to shark diving as part of an organized group rather than doing it alone. Apart from the fact that it is more fun to be in the company of like-minded people, it has the benefit of an experienced tour leader with local knowledge and the ability to smooth out occasional difficulties during the trip. It can also be considerably cheaper, making boat charters and cage hire more economical.

Before you leave home, ensure that your equipment is complete and in perfect working order. If you do not dive regularly, it is a good idea to have a practice beforehand, or at least do a check-out dive with the dive master as soon as you arrive. This will enable you to check all your gear, and will refresh your basic diving skills. Too many divers wait until they are inside a shark cage or on the sea floor surrounded by sharks to realize that their masks are leaking or their weight belts are too light. All dive operators require proof of certification, so take your dive card with you. On advanced dives you may be required to show your dive log to demonstrate that you are adequately experienced.

Finally, insurance is another important consideration. You may not be covered by your normal insurance if you dive with sharks. A good source of advice is the American-based diving insurance and accident management service, the Divers Alert Network, which has an inexpensive annual membership fee. In the USA and Canada contact dan@diversalertnetwork.org; in Europe contact mail@daneurope.org; and in Southeast Asia and the Pacific contact danseap@danseap.org.

When you have chosen your preferred shark species and dive site, selected a suitable operator, checked your equipment and had a practice dive... finally, you are ready to meet the sharks face to face. There are a few simple guidelines to follow under water, which will help to make the dive safe and more enjoyable.

The dive master will brief you on the sharks you are about to encounter, and will explain how to act during the dive. Follow the instructions carefully, especially if you are joining an organized feed. The sharks are used to a certain routine, and if the pattern changes, they may become confused. Never dive with sharks alone, and never be fooled by operators who pretend that they are no more dangerous than playful puppies. The most experienced

Opposite: Cage-diving off the coast of Guadalupe,
Mexico – a hotspot for great white sharks.
Overleaf: Snorkelling with a giant whale shark off
the coast of western Australia.

shark divers always retain a healthy respect for every species. It is largely a matter of common sense.

Cage dives are perhaps the safest way to encounter sharks, although they have their own inherent risks. Most cages are not shark-proof, but merely provide a tactile and visual barrier between the sharks and the divers, and they often have gaps for photography that are large enough to permit small sharks to enter – and small sharks really do enter more often than you might imagine. Some cage dives also involve swimming, unprotected, through open water to get into and out of the cage.

In many cases, the sharks will be as frightened of you as you are of them. Try to avoid intimidating them: stay still or move very slowly, and slow your breathing to minimize the noise from your exhaust bubbles. If you feel it is safe to get closer, swim on a converging course rather than in a direct line. When the sharks feel confident, they may approach you instead. They are naturally inquisitive animals, so if this happens, do not assume that you are in trouble...and try not to panic. After all, a real-life close encounter with one of the most beautiful, intelligent and mysterious creatures on Earth is why you jumped into the sea in the first place – and it is certainly something you will never forget.

Where to see sharks

There are nearly 300 recognized shark-watching hotspots around the world, and between them they offer the chance to have a close encounter with a wide variety of sharks, ranging from great whites and sand tigers to silvertips and whale sharks. Here is a small selection to illustrate the impressive variety of face-to-face encounters possible.

1 USA: North Carolina

Papoose, *Caribsea* and *Atlas* wrecks, 50 km (32 miles) south of Cape Lookout; nearest town Morehead City

Main species: Sand tiger shark

Best time of year: The sharks are present all year round, but the best diving is from June to September.

Contact details: Diveocean Dive Center (www.divocean-dive-center.com); Diver Down (www.diverdownscubadiving.com); Pelican Divers Inc (www.diveguideint.com/p0408a.htm).

The treacherous waters along the North Carolina coastline are world-renowned for wreck diving, and provide divers with a rare opportunity to explore a four-century-long chronicle of maritime history. This area is also one of the best places in the world to see sand tiger sharks. These fierce-looking sharks, characterized by row after row of needle-sharp teeth, are a familiar sight at several wrecks in the area. Traditionally they congregated around the *Papoose* (an oil tanker sunk by a German torpedo in 1942), probably using it as both a feeding and breeding area. But recently they have been more common around the *Atlas* and *Caribsea* wrecks, and can also be seen at several other wrecks along this stretch of coast. The sand tigers regard divers with idle curiosity, frequently approaching to within 1 m (3 feet) or so, but show no sign of aggression.

2 Canada: British Columbia

Hornby Island in the Strait of Georgia, midway between Nanaimo and Campbell River, off the east coast of Vancouver Island

Main species: Bluntnose sixgill shark

Best time of year: May to September

Contact details: Hornby Island Diving (www.hornbyislanddiving.com); Ocean Explorers Diving (www.oceanexplorersdiving.com)

Bluntnose sixgill sharks are widely distributed around the world, but there are few places where it is possible to view them. Adults

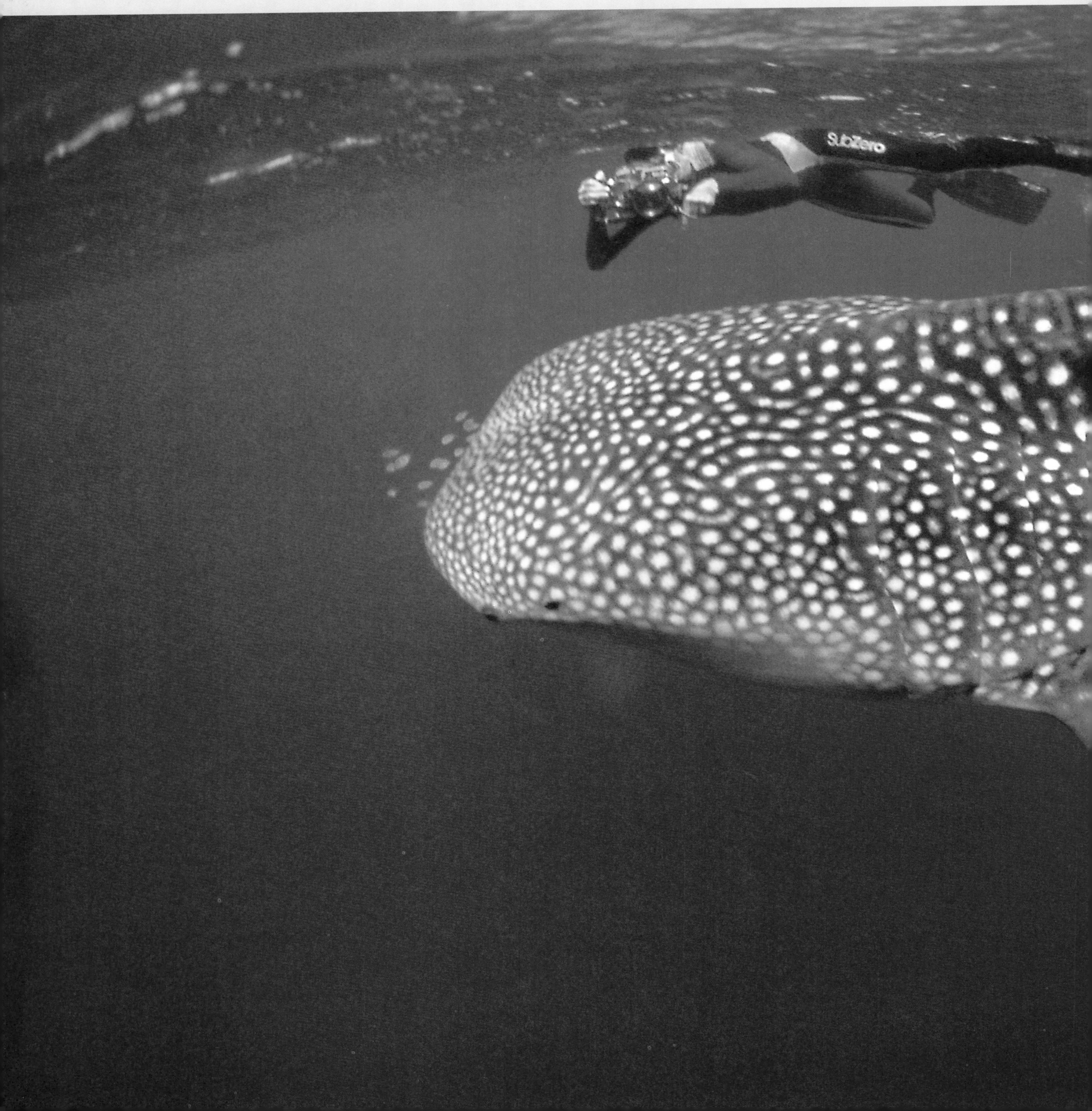
SubZero

are usually found at great depth – up to 2500 m (8200 feet) – so are inaccessible to people under most circumstances. Juveniles are more likely to be found inshore, and one particular population, which makes a brief appearance in the Pacific northwest every summer, frequently ventures into much shallower water. At Flora Islet, next to Hornby Island, they are commonly seen at depths of 40 m (130 feet) or less, and at night have even been reported as shallow as 10 m (33 feet). This puts them well within reach of recreational divers. More sixgills can be found at depths of 120–220 m (400–700 feet) throughout the summer, and for a few years there was a unique opportunity at Hornby Island to view them from deep-water submersibles. The submersible dives have been discontinued, but scuba diving with the sharks is still popular.

Below: The Basking Shark Society runs trips to observe and snorkel with basking sharks around the Isle of Man, midway between mainland Britain and Ireland.

3 Mexico: Guadalupe Island

Guadalupe Island, 340 km (210 miles) south-southwest of San Diego

Main species: Great white shark

Best time of year: The sharks are present from August to at least January, but the shark-watching trips are conducted in September, October and November

Contact details: San Diego Shark Diving Expeditions (www.sdsharkdiving.com/guadalupe.htm); Horizon Charters (www.horizoncharters.com)

Better known for its native population of rare fur seals, the remote island of Guadalupe is a relatively new shark-diving destination. It has long had a reputation as a haven for great white sharks, but the first of many proposed cage-diving trips did not take place until the autumn of 2001. It is now considered to be among a handful of places around the world where great whites can be seen on a regular basis. Two large four-person cages

are suspended at the surface from the back of the boat, and the sharks are attracted with the help of chum. It is not unusual to have several large individuals milling around at once, and the visibility is usually excellent, typically 24–30 m (80–100 feet).

4 Costa Rica: Cocos Island

480–600 km (300–375 miles) southwest of the Pacific coast of Costa Rica

Main species: Scalloped hammerhead

Best time of year: The hammerheads are present all year round

Contact details: *Undersea Hunter* and *Sea Hunter* (www.underseahunter.com); *Okeanos Aggressor* (www.aggressor.com); HMS *The New Inzan Tiger* (www.theinzantiger.com); Scuba Tours Worldwide (www.scubascuba.com)

Cocos Island is a challenging dive location and, as shark photographer Jeff Rotman once commented, the 'shark equivalent of Piccadilly Circus'. It is often claimed that there are more sharks per cubic metre here than anywhere else on Earth. Sharks of one species or another are encountered on virtually every dive, frequently in breathtaking numbers. Whitetip reef, silky, silvertip and blacktip sharks are all common, but scalloped hammerheads are the local speciality. They form an ever-present backdrop to many dives (especially at Manuelita, Alcyone and Dirty Rock). In fact, Cocos is one of the few places in the world where it is possible to dive among literally hundreds of hammerheads. Although they are notoriously skittish and easily spooked, if you have a little knowledge and patience, close encounters are virtually guaranteed.

5 The Bahamas: Grand Bahama Island

Shark Junction, 3 km (2 miles) offshore from Port Lucaya, near Freeport

Main species: Caribbean reef shark

Best time of year: The sharks are present all year round

Contact details: UNEXSO (www.unexso.com)

Shark Junction is the site of one of the best-known and most popular shark feeds in the world. The Underwater Explorers Society (UNEXSO) has been feeding as many as 30 Caribbean reef sharks here every day since the late 1980s. Approximately a dozen divers descend to the sandy seabed, at a depth of about 14 m (45 feet), and kneel in a wide semicircle with their backs against a rusty old decompression chamber. They are accompanied by four dive masters: an underwater videographer, two safety divers, who keep a watchful eye on proceedings, and a professional shark feeder. The sharks swim around the feeder (who wears a protective chain-mail suit) and, one by one, he (or she) literally hands entire herring or mackerel to each one in turn. As well as Caribbean reef sharks, nurse sharks are also frequent visitors to this underwater banquet.

6 Britain: Isle of Man

Irish Sea, midway between mainland Britain and Ireland

Main species: Basking shark

Best time of year: The sharks are present and the weather is at its best from mid-May to September

Contact details: Basking Shark Society (www.isle-of-man.com/interests/shark/index.htm)

The Isle of Man is home to one of the largest concentrations of basking sharks anywhere in the world. It is not unusual to have several animals in view at once, and large groups of more than 50 are occasionally seen during organized trips. The sharks spend much of their time at the surface, and some individuals come right alongside the boat, with their mouths wide open, so these tours offer one of the few shark-watching opportunities for young children and non-swimmers. If conditions permit, confident swimmers are allowed to enter the water to snorkel with the relatively harmless animals as they feed no more than a metre or two away – one of the world's greatest wildlife encounters.

7 The Phillipines: Sorsogon

Donsol, in the Burias Strait in western Sorsogon; approximately 400 km (250 miles) southeast of Manila

Main species: Whale shark

Best time of year: The sharks are present from November until June, although the numbers usually peak in March

Contact details: WWF Philippines (www.wwf-phil.com.ph); Philippines Department of Tourism (www.tourism.gov.ph); Dive Elite (www.diveelite.com/whaletour.html); Kalinga Travel Adventure (www.ktadventure.com/kta_enver/whale_en.htm)

The huge gathering of whale sharks at the mouth of the Donsol River had been known to the small coastal community of Donsol for generations, but the outside world did not hear about it until 1997. The sharks gather in the area for about six months every year to feed in the plankton-rich waters, and this is one of the few places in the world where they can easily be spotted in large numbers. Shark watching here is centrally co-ordinated and conducted under strict guidelines. Shark watchers pay a fee and are given a research kit (WWF-Philippines runs a voluntary research programme and asks everyone to help in gathering data) before being assigned to a boat. Each boat has six passengers on board, together with an official spotter (who may once have been a whale shark fisherman) and the skipper. The boat positions itself a few metres ahead of the shark, then the snorkellers ease themselves quietly into the water for a thrilling close encounter.

8 New Zealand: North Island

Hawkes Bay, 3–13 km (2–8 miles) off the coast of Napier, on the east coast of central North Island

Main species: Blue shark and shortfin mako

Best time of year: The sharks are present from November until March, although the best months are January and February

Contact details: Dive HQ Napier (www.divehq.co.nz)

Better known for its award-winning wines, Hawkes Bay is also a good place for sharks. Blues and makos migrate to the region with the warm-water currents each summer, and can readily be seen at three different open-water sites. Chum is used to attract the sharks, and bait stations are set up close to the cage, which floats at the surface in water approximately 100 m (330 feet) deep. There is no hand-feeding. Four divers can enter the cage or, if they prefer, can swim with the sharks in open water nearby. It normally takes about half an hour for the sharks to appear on a typical dive, and between six and 12 of them turn up on most days. They approach very closely, and the blues will even brush against divers outside the cage.

9 Australia: Western Australia

Kalbarri, 10 km (6 miles) offshore at the mouth of the Murchison River; approximately 600 km (370 miles) north of Perth

Main species: Bronze whaler and blacktip sharks

Best time of year: The sharks are present from November until June, but the best weather is usually during March, April and May

Contact details: Kalbarri Explorer Ocean Charters (www.kalbarriexplorer.com.au)

Shark watching in Kalbarri is unique. There is nothing else quite like it in the world. Large numbers of bronze whaler and blacktip sharks are virtually guaranteed – and you do not even have to get your feet wet. The sharks habitually follow cray-fishing boats to feed on the leftover bait from their pots, and, by special arrangement, a catamaran full of shark watchers is allowed to come along to watch the spectacle. On average, six to 12 sharks

follow each cray boat, and because they do not make a distinction, they follow the catamaran as well. They swim within metres of the boat and will even lift their heads out of the water to take food.

10 French Polynesia: Rangiroa Atoll

Avatoru Pass and Tiputa Pass, 330 km (205 miles) northeast of Tahiti in the Tuamotu archipelago

Main species: Grey reef, whitetip reef, blacktip reef and silvertip sharks

Best time of year: Most sharks are present all year round, but the best diving conditions are from September to early November

Contact details: Raie Manta Club (www.raiemantaclub.free.fr); The Six Passengers Diving Center (www.the6passengers.com/anglais) Dream Dive (www.dreamdive.pf); Rangiroa Paradive (www.chez.com/paradive); Manihi Blue Nui Dive Center (www.bluenui.com)

Dubbed by many as the Shark Capital of the South Pacific, Rangiroa more than lives up to its reputation. The inner lagoon of the atoll opens to the Pacific through two passes: Tiputa and Avatoru. Fast-flowing tidal currents rush through these narrow openings in the reef, and are home to bewildering numbers of sharks of several different species. Tiputa has more sharks, but Avatoru is particularly good for silvertips. Divers are propelled through the passes at great speed in the company of dozens or even hundreds of sharks, and few dives are more exhilarating. Once described as like flying out of control with a gang of accommodating Hell's Angels, the experience is not for the faint-hearted.

Above: Diving with a silvertip shark at Rangiroa Atoll in French Polynesia.

164

Further reading

The Complete Idiot's Guide to Sharks, Mary L. Peachin, Pearson Education Inc, USA, 2003

Diving with Sharks and Other Adventure Dives, Jack Jackson, New Holland Publishers, London, 2000

The Encyclopedia of Sharks, Steve and Jane Parker, Firefly Books, London, 2002

Great White Sharks: The Biology of Carcharodon carcharias, A. Peter Klimley and David G. Ainley (eds), Academic Press, San Diego, 1996

In Depth Adventure Guides: Red Sea Sharks, Jeremy Stafford-Deitsch, Trident Press, London, 1999

The Private Life of Sharks: The Truth Behind the Myth, Michael Bright, Robson Books, London, 1999

Shark!, Jeffrey L. Rotman, Ipso Facto Publishers, Paris, 1999

Sharks, Michael Bright, The Natural History Museum, London, 2002

Sharks and Rays, Doug Perrine, Colin Baxter Photography Ltd, Grantown-on-Spey, 1999

Sharks & Rays: The Ultimate Guide to Underwater Predators, Leighton Taylor (consultant editor), HarperCollins, London, 1997

Sharks in Danger: Global Shark Conservation Status with Reference to Management Plans and Legislation, Rachel Cunningham-Day, Universal Publishers, Parkland (USA), 2001

Sharks in Question: The Smithsonian Answer Book, Victor G. Springer and Joy P. Gold, Smithsonian Institution Press, Washington, DC, 1989

Sharks: The Mysterious Killers, Downs Matthews, Discovery Channel Books, New Jersey, 1996

Shark Trouble, Peter Benchley, Random House, New York, 2002

The Shark Watcher's Handbook, Mark Carwardine and Ken Watterson, BBC Worldwide Ltd, London, 2002

Index

Page numbers in *italics* indicate illustrations and captions.

Acknowledgements

This book could not have been written without a great deal of effort from a large number of people. I am indebted to everyone at BBC Books, in particular Shirley Patton, Trish Burgess, Frances Abraham, Julie Tochel and Annette Peppis. It has been a great pleasure working with them, and their patience, enthusiasm, encouragement and professionalism have been an inspiration. Over the years, many dive operators and shark experts have introduced me to sharks in some wonderful places around the world and have willingly shared their knowledge. I would like to thank them all for their generosity, insight and friendship.

Picture credits

BBC Worldwide would like to thank the following for providing photographs and for permission to reproduce copyright material. While every effort has been made to trace and acknowledge all copyright holders, we would like to apologize for any errors or omissions, and invite readers to inform us so that corrections can be made in any future editions of the book.

American Museum of Natural History, Courtesy of Dept. of Library Services 28; **Mark Carwardine** 23, 71, 97, 107, 116, 151 *top*, 156 & 160; **Brandon D. Cole** 16 *left*; **Corbis** 11 & 98; **Corbis/Bettmann** 92; **Corbis/Sygma/Brecels** 121; **FLPA** Mark Newman 94, Flip Nicklin/Minden Pictures 102–3 *centre*, Tershy/Strong/Earthviews 35; **Getty Images** 79 & 128; **Ronald Grant Archive/Universal Pictures** 12; **Alan James** 80; **Lochman Transparencies** Clay Bryce 84–5; **Natural Visions** 118 *bottom*; **Nature Picture Library** Jürgen Freund 1, Avi Klapfer/Jeff Rotman Photography 3 *right*, 13 *main picture*, Bruce Rasner/Jeff Rotman Photography 141, Jeff Rotman 19, 49, 112, 139, 143, 144, 150 & 154; **NHPA** ANT Photo Library 2–3 left, 10 & 14, Norbert Wu 54–5 & 123; **OSF** Mark Deeble & Victoria Stone 46, David Fleetham 52 & 64, Howard Hall 142, Tammy Peluso 89, Norbert Wu 13 *inset*; **Rex** 93; **Science Photo Library/Eye of Science** 36; **Seapics.com** Kurt Amsler 131, Gary Bell 149, Jonathan Bird 40, Jeffrey C. Carrier 65, Mark Conlin 5, 58 & 151 *bottom*, Bob Cranston 8, 17, 20, 72 & 74, Ben Cropp Productions 75 & 104, C. & M. Fallows 6 & 76, Howard Hall 41 & 67, Bill Harrigan 135 & 137, Richard Herrmann 50, Chris Huss 61, Jeffrey Jaskolski 43, Michel Jozon 62, Marilyn Kazmers 117, 148 & 153, Maris & Marilyn Kazmers 82–3, Nigel Marsh 86, Amos Nachoum 101, Michael S. Nolan 15 & 56, Doug Perrine 16 *right*, 22, 32, 44, 69, 102 *left*, 103 *right*, 111, 115, 124–5, 132, 136, 140, 155 & 163, Jeff Rotman 147, Norine Rouse 63, André Seale 138, David Shen 29, Marty Snyderman 34 & 77, Mark Strickland 39 & 70, Masa Ushioda 30 & 47, James D. Watt 90 & 108; **Still Pictures** Fred Bavendam 158–9, Roland Seitre 120, Dino Simeonidis 126, Norbert Wu 118 *top* & *centre*.